A BETTER WAY OUT

When You Feel Like Giving Up

Glena Sue Fitzmorris

A BETTER WAY OUT: When You Feel Like Giving Up

©2021 by Glena Sue Fitzmorris

All rights reserved. No part of this book may be reproduced or transmitted in any form or by any means, electronic or mechanical, including photocopying, recording or by any information storage and retrieval system, without permission in writing from the copyright owner.

All scriptures, unless otherwise indicated, are taken from the *King James Version* of the Bible.

Scripture quotations marked (AMP) are taken from the Amplified® Bible, Copyright © 1954, 1958, 1962, 1964, 1965, 1987 by The Lockman Foundation. Used by permission. (www.Lockman.org)

Scripture quotations marked (AMP) are taken from *The Amplified Bible,* Old Testament. Copyright © 1965, 1987, by the Zondervan Corporation. Used by permission. All rights reserved.

Scripture quotations marked (AMPC) are taken from *The Amplified Bible*, Classic Edition. Copyright © 1954, 1958, 1962, 1964, 1965, 1987 by The Lockman Foundation. Used by permission. All rights reserved.

Scripture quotations marked (CEV) are taken from the *Contemporary English Version* © 1991, 1992, 1995, by American Bible Society. Used by permission. All rights reserved.

Scripture quotations marked (CSB) are taken from The Christian Standard Bible. Copyright © 2017 by Holman Bible Publishers. Used by permission. Christian Standard Bible® and CSB® are federally registered trademarks of Holman Bible Publishers, all rights reserved.

Scripture quotations marked (ESV) are taken from the ESV® Bible (The Holy Bible, English Standard Version®), copyright © 2001 by Crossway, a publishing ministry of Good News Publishers. Used by permission. All rights reserved.

Scripture quotations marked (MEV) are taken from the Modern English Version. Copyright © 2014 by Military Bible Association. Used by permission. All rights reserved.

Scripture quotations marked (MSG) are taken from *THE MESSAGE.* Copyright © by Eugene H. Peterson 1993, 1994, 1995, 1996, 2000, 2001, 2002. Used by permission of NavPress Publishing Group.

Scripture quotations marked (NASB) are taken from the New American Standard Bible®, Copyright © 1960, 1962, 1963, 1968, 1971, 1972, 1973, 1975, 1977, 1995 by The Lockman Foundation. Used by permission. (www.Lockman.org)

Scripture quotations marked (NCV) are taken from the New Century Version®. Copyright © 1987, 1988, 1991 by Word Publishing, a division of Thomas Nelson, Inc. Used by permission. All rights reserved.

Scripture quotations marked (NIV) are taken from the Holy Bible, New International Version®, NIV®. Copyright © 1973, 1978, 1984, 2011 by Biblica, Inc.™ Used by permission of Zondervan. All rights reserved worldwide. www.zondervan.com
The "NIV" and "New International Version" are trademarks registered in the United States Patent and Trademark Office by Biblica, Inc.™

Scripture quotations marked (NKJV) are taken from the New King James Version®. Copyright © 1982 by Thomas Nelson. Used by permission. All rights reserved.

Scripture quotations marked (NLV) are taken from the New Life Version. Copyright © 1969, 2003 by Barbour Publishing, Inc. Used by permission. All rights reserved.

Scripture quotations marked (NLT) are taken from the Holy Bible, New Living Translation, copyright © 1996, 2004, 2007 by Tyndale House Foundation. Used by permission of Tyndale House Publishers, Inc., Carol Stream, Illinois 60188. All rights reserved.

Scripture quotations marked (TLB) are taken from The Living Bible copyright © 1971. Used by permission of Tyndale House Publishers, Inc., Carol Stream, Illinois 60188. All rights reserved.

Scripture quotations marked (VOICE) are taken from *The Voice*. The Voice Bible Copyright © 2012 Thomas Nelson, Inc. The Voice™ translation © 2012 Ecclesia Bible Society. Used by permission. All rights reserved.

Disclaimer: The contents of this book are not intended as a substitute for professional help, such as counseling, psychiatric treatment, and other medical intervention. The author shall not be held liable or responsible for anyone who chooses suicide. As expressed in the book, the author heartily encourages professional help, while this book may serve to complement such therapy.

Published by GSF Books, Lumberton, Texas.

Cover and Interior Design by Suzanne Lawing.

Distribution and Printing Services by Believers Book Services, Colorado Springs, CO.

Printed in the United States of America.

978-0-578-31450-1

Dedication

First and foremost, I commit this work into the hands of Jesus before it lands in the hands of anyone else. It is for each reader's life that He died to save and rescue from the jaws of suicide. His love pulsates strongly throughout these pages, which I pray each reader experiences in a life-changing way.

Although my mom is with Jesus now, having finished her race after battling cancer with such grace through immeasurable suffering, I honor her by dedicating this book to her. She knew about this project before she died and had encouraged me to finish it. Had it not been for her prayers for me to conquer this temptation of suicide, I would not be alive today, let alone have written these words to encourage others that they can overcome the same internal conflict as well.

CONTENTS

Introduction 9

SECTION ONE

Internal War 13
A Quest for Comforting Presence 15
Grief-Stricken 17
Freedom Comes with Needing 19
The Wind and Waves Obey Him 21
Time to Live Again 23
From the Depths I Cry Out 25
Suddenly 27
Hope 29

SECTION TWO

Does My Life Have Value? 33
The Dead Can't Think Ahead 41
Peace Is Possible 49
The Mastermind of Evil 57
Life After Failure 63
Giving the "What If" a Chance 71
Your Shift Is Coming 77
The "I" in S-u-I-c-I-d-e 83

Outsiders and Outcasts 93
Door to Hope: Finding a Friend Who Never Fails 101
Invalidation 111
Giving Away Our Power 119
Tracing the "I Theme" 127
Death of a Different Kind 141
Coming Out of the Darkness 153
In God We Trust—or Not 165
His Wounds Have Paid Our Ransom 175
Every Life Matters 183
Last Days 189
The Guaranteed Way Out 193

SECTION THREE

Prayer for Salvation 209
Notes to the Others Involved 211
About the Author 215

INTRODUCTION

With the pressures we are all facing, living through such turbulent chaos of unprecedented times and undeniable signs of the End Times, suicide rates are on the rise. People from all walks of life may find themselves frantically searching for hope and a reason to keep living. Life can really hurt sometimes, often more than it seems we can bear. Teenagers feel the pressures to conform, plagued with inadequacy of not measuring up. Failed marriages leave spouses grappling with questions, such as how can they possibly start over now, or even how to go on at all? Singles, addicts, or the abused feel trapped in isolation, tempted to believe their disappearance wouldn't even matter. The small business owner with a dream buried in ashes, whose venture has failed, now struggles with paying bills, and is ready to quit on life altogether. The elderly, who never wanted to be a burden, have added heartache in coping with the volatility of our times. Even pastors of churches are not immune, as the enemy has pressed and pushed in fierce fashion tempting them to give up too.

The heavy weight of suicide temptation has no favorites; it will target even the best. In fact, the mastermind of evil discerns you have tremendous potential, created for a unique purpose only you can fulfill. It's why he's threatened by you and seeks to take you out. Take heart, my friend, you are not alone. As you reach for hope, you will find it. This may be your darkest night of the soul, but holding this book puts you in the right place at the right time. Find the heart of God beating strong with love for you; He has plenty hope to give you. There is no condemnation here.

While our current events may present to be the "last straw" for you, this book is not focused on such upheavals as the coronavirus pandemic, violent riots, economic swings, or politics at all. It transcends to a deeper level as a message of lasting hope in the midst of all that. Whereas suicide temptation convinces you there is no other way out, these pages prove that there is, in fact, a better way out than suicide.

Thus, you will find it to be not a textbook style of scientific, psychological data and statistics; nor will you find judgment of any kind. Hope, mercy, and redemption run full course as the theme to help you live again. You may be on the fence, not so sure you want that yet. You may be hurting to such depths that pain has obscured your view of God or clouded the reality of His love, tainting your perception that He is only harsh and punishing, or some other distancing falsehood. You may oppressively wrestle with seeing Him for Who He really is.

In the wintry lows of soul and seasons of discouragement, the love of God will go the distance to rescue, help, and save us even from ourselves. This is a book grounded in personal experience, as I was also painfully crushed in the jaws of suicide temptation for a prolonged period of time. Therefore, I write from an overflow of compassion for you, straight from the Father's heart, Who longs for you to experience His love with no trace of shame whatsoever.

Follow me first to the opening pages where I share from my own poetic sketches when I was walking through the valley of death's shadow. Time after time, tempted to take my own life, the encounters of God's truth triumphantly prevailed. Pain in my heart became an instrument in my Redeemer's hands to play a melody of hope for other hurting lives. Hopefully, you will feel from the start an immediate connection; and see that it is a book not written "at" you, but truly "for" you. My prayer is that you will find the truth that sets you free and the hope that comes when you choose life.

SECTION ONE

INTERNAL WAR

Brace yourself. Your enemy has studied you for a long time—all your life! The mastermind of evil has been stalking you at your weakest moments, and even more dangerously, the times you've felt strong. He expertly knows your weaknesses and vulnerabilities, craftily setting traps and pitfalls along your path.

Even so, "Take heart!" Jesus said, "I have overcome the world" (John 16:33 ESV). Whose voice will you heed? Lean in closer to the Savior, Who only speaks the language of love and truth. No other power is greater; we know how the story ends.

You know what those times are like, how the darkness closes in on you. The seething self-hatred, remorse, and regrets plague your mind while trying to rest. They come with fierce strength and opposition. You recognize it by the way it creeps upon you when you weren't looking—much like an attacker peering through one's window waiting for his theft opportunity.

Whether the latch was left unlocked because of bitterness, anger, unforgiveness, and all the self-loathing, one thing is clear—it granted wide-open access to the enemy of your soul.

As God told Cain, so He tells us the same today, "Sin crouches at your door; its desire is for you [to overpower you], but you must master it" (Genesis 4:7 AMP). This same sin has "wages" of death, "but the gift of God is eternal life in Christ Jesus our Lord" (Romans 6:23 NIV).

Sin is the job; death is the paycheck. No wonder the dark enemy of your soul pushes and pressures you into suicide, as if there is no other way out. He tempted you and down you fell. Now he demands your debts be paid in punishment by taking your own life.

Yet Jesus has spoken that His Blood speaks a better word than the vengeance you seek against yourself. "This is My Blood, a covenant poured out on behalf of many" (Mark 14:26 VOICE). It was so that you can be forgiven. Atonement was made for your sin debt, stamped as "Paid in Full."

"Forgive," Jesus whispers.

"But I can't!" argued the wounded heart.

"Yes, you can. Because I forgave you, you can forgive too, even when that person is you."

A QUEST FOR COMFORTING PRESENCE

God, are You even there at all?
        The walls are closing in on me.
The night is growing darker.
        Hope is but a long lost dream.
I haven't any sense of You—Your love, comfort, or presence.
        As the moon that slips behind heavy, dark storm clouds,
Your face is hidden when I need You most.

In these darkest of nights,
        where do You go?
I have seemingly lost my way
        while others go on busily about each day.
Occupied with friends and family—"togetherness" a theme,
        I feel so lost and alone
Always marching to the beat of a different drum.

Despair has been my closest friend
        though I'd pay it to leave if I could.
All the money in the world combined
        wouldn't make a dent in that possibility
You're the only One Who holds the keys
        to my freedom from this prison—my release.

GRIEF-STRICKEN

The most unbelievably dark night of the soul imaginable, my worst nightmare has occurred.

Thoughts of suicide had pounded in my head in an ongoing dull manner for quite some time, but tonight was somehow different.

Fierce, strong, resounding, and repetitively piercing are the pains of such tormenting thoughts.

Inevitably, imminent death looms in my vision. Tears are flowing as madness in frantic, desperate search of all that could be wrong in such a surface kind of way.

Though plenty comes to mind, as a depressed soul never has to look far, wide, or long for troubling reasons and terribly sad scapegoats on which to blame the present darkness, the longer I stare deeper into the moonlit iridescent mini-blinds, the wider my eyes become with the stinging blow of reality.

A much deeper, penetrating pain it is than even all my circling fears for months over surface matters that have been shouting despair.

It is stronger than even my constant concerns about the future. Now, it is simply one more day I cannot face.

Paralyzing and shattering to the core of my being, suddenly it strikes me by force how severely profound this loss has changed me, knocking the wind of hope far from me.

A permanent ink blot never to be removed. History has been made without the hope of a re-do, with only regrets as all I have left. As soon as I start nursing those, however, they grow into monsters of evil tormenting woe.

As torrential floodwaters overwhelm an entire town that is unprepared for disaster, these regrets, longings, and grief pangs begin filling every crevice of my heart, soul, mind—indeed my entire being—quicker than I can release tears or express such intense sorrow through writing, or any other desperately frantic, coping strategy.

Tossing, turning, writhing in the depths of pain and sorrow—oh Heavenly Father, are You even there, or have You left as well?

Like David said, "My soul refuses to be comforted."[1] Nevertheless, I endeavor to give You a tiny piece of belief. It is all I have, but my only last hope is to believe in You, that You have promised never to leave or forsake me.[2]

Though hurting to the core of my heart and soul, I have but one resolve to keep believing; so help my unbelief.

---

1 Psalm 77:2

2 Hebrews 13:5-6

FREEDOM COMES WITH NEEDING

Far away from everyone
        is where my body sought to go.
I used to think my soul agreed;
        instead my spirit fought with me.
People everywhere I've shunned;
        I thought I needed no one.
Now, much to my surprise I see
        that having friends has set me free.
Because in Your Body I have found
        a bond is formed where there's common ground.
At the foot of the Cross where Your Blood poured out
        where in unity—a home for my heart—is found.

THE WIND AND WAVES OBEY HIM

Waves of tumult and confusion roar within my soul just as the tide rushes to the shore so loudly. Even the boulders, stable and buried within the sand, are overtaken by the water's power.

Likewise, I am overwhelmed by the crashing of these waves of despair within my soul. Rather than the sun's glistening illumination upon the ocean waves, a darkened shadow is cast upon those that encroach upon my heart.

Still the fury, still the crashing, still the roaring thunder-like sound, but oh so different in their landing places.

Those upon the shore recede by ebb and flow as the beautiful way of the sea; whereas those that crash against my soul fall with a giant thud, blanketing me with heaviness that remains and won't recede.

The undercurrent of hope becomes too weak to pull them back into the sea of despondency, where they belong—away from me.

Ah, but in the loving-kindness of Your creation, You allow both the high tide and recession to occur. Indeed, You have ordained each detail to manifest Your glory and demonstrate Your power.

As the wind and waves of the sea obey Your Voice, they rise and fall at Your command; so can You speak to the storm raging within me.

Lord Jesus, when You were sleeping in a boat with Your disciples, this same stormy blast of wind and waves rattled You not. The mighty uproar shook the boat in violent tempest, but Your Words made all the difference.

Simply by divine authority of Who You are, You commanded, "Peace, be still." With no other strategy needed, the wind and waves acquiesced and silenced immediately.

Ah, Lord God Almighty, the same yesterday, today, and forever, the wind and waves of all kinds *still* obey You.

Thus, I humbly ask You, as Your child with a raging storm inside my soul, please speak, "Peace, be still." For these winds and waves within me will hear Your Voice and obey.

You promised us this perfect peace my insides are craving to receive. As You have spoken, so shall it be.

TIME TO LIVE AGAIN

It is supposedly the turning of a New Year.
    Nothing in the natural has changed.
Even so, I am so weary of dying from this loss.
    The decaying process of merely existing has taken such a heavy, taxing toll.
The words I heard pierced my soul like a fiery knife.
    It is time to live again.
Would this not make me a traitor? Ah, my love is so loyal.
    No, to live by choice would make me a brave warrior.
Teased into thinking I am living by barely existing
    is but a lie to keep me empty and fruitless.
Awake, my soul! Death has held you captive for way too long;
    the pain of loss was in the casket.
God, quite honestly, I still don't understand why;
    but I resolve that even if I did, the pain would not subside.
You have the power to raise the dead.
    Yes, I believe in You this much.
Yet I also believe You are utterly creative
    to bring life into my deadness in any other way.
So, I lift up my eyes beyond the heavens
    "from whence cometh my help"[1]
I open my hands and raise them high
    it all begins with no longer having to understand why.

I surrender all in order to go forward;
> I must release the past of all I have loved.

Not that I stop loving,
> but that in living again, I embrace the joy of that sweet reunion someday.

---

1 Psalm 121:1b

FROM THE DEPTHS
I CRY OUT

Peace for this racing, dizzying status of mind, when all within me fights for a way out.
    Grant me Your staying power; I am lost without You.

Guidance for the overwhelming myriad of tasks, when all I can do is blankly stare at the list
    Of all there is to do without the energy to carry it through.

Solutions for the puzzling questions debilitating my dreams,
    Or the capacity to trust You without answers when they seem unfulfilled.

Hope for the moments threatening my vision,
    To increase my faith in the looming shadows of fear.

Endurance for the journey when the road seems to lengthen,
    Courage for a strong identity in You; Your Word is my only Truth.

Above all, teach me to love in the midst of the pain
    In spite of the questions, in the face of each fear.

These three remain: faith, hope, and love,
 But the greatest of these is Love.

Dread has no place
 Your Perfect Love casts out all fear.

SUDDENLY

Countless years spent in the dry, barren wastelands. No successes to show, only sorrows. Immeasurable time spent in agonizing grief, turmoil, misery, despair, and emotional pain untold.

One touch from the Master's hand upon my shoulder came. The powerful surge of the name of Jesus breathed fresh new life into these darkened places of pain, "Dry bones, Live!"

That is when I knew deliverance had come. How very long it had been, all swept away in a moment by a miraculous "Suddenly" from Him.

Chains had been binding me for so long that I was quite accustomed to the tightness of their grip in my innermost parts.

The tension, the stress headaches, the cramped muscles rigid with anxiety, the extremities of fear disabling my sleep; and oh the pressures to conform crushing all my creativity.

Ah, but as the song was being sung in my spirit, I began to hear the sweetest name of all—Jesus. Without a second thought, I extended my hands as He was drawing closer.

I felt every bit as needy and languishing in spirit as the man beside the Pool of Bethesda. Surely I could hear Him say, "Do you *want* to be made whole?"

Before I caught myself, my reply sounded just like that man at first—full of excuses as to why I was stuck and could not move beyond my plight.

Poised for condemnation, all I found instead was His voice of mercy, deliverance, healing, and love. Feeling so undeserving, the grace in His eyes I could not refuse.

Overlooking my awkward, imperfect response, He chose to hear my cry and meet my need, healing me in spite of the weaknesses He saw in me.

His bold proclamation: "Rise up and walk" has not changed! The waters are being stirred, and it is time to jump into the cool refreshing for newness of life to begin.

He still speaks the same today. Do you hear Him drawing you near? "Rise up and walk," your "Suddenly" is here!

Newfound strength for the journey, no more dreading each day. Courage for tomorrow, the race is not over.

Slowly it starts, then "Suddenly" it happens. No shadow of turning with Jesus; He never changes. His love is the constant no matter the chaos. So I gave Him my heart.

Out of the ashes, arise, my soul, with hope! This is just the beginning of knowing Who Jesus really is, the One Who with just one touch has made me whole.

HOPE

Herein lies the hope:
Your Word has the final say.

Herein lies the hope:
On the Cross, You said, "It is Finished!"

Herein lies the hope:
Your mercies are new every morning.

Herein lies the hope:
Your promises never fail.

Herein lies the hope:
The Blood of Jesus is sufficient.

Herein lies the hope:
Your opinion is all that matters.

Herein lies the hope:
You, my Lord, have said I'm forgiven.

SECTION TWO

DOES MY LIFE HAVE VALUE?

A pastor I once had shared a powerful story about his past days as a young man while working on the docking area of Port Neches, Texas when the historical explosion occurred. When he vulnerably exposed this experience of his, it gave me a tangible example to use in expressing how your life—as one individual—matters greatly to God.

In his late teens, he had already left work for his particular shift, while several members of his crew remained on the dock just hanging out, as the guys often did. As he was driving away, he turned his head and literally saw the explosion take place, smoky fumes filling the air and lives suddenly in perilous danger. Hurriedly making his way back to help his coworkers, and rescue as many men who were drowning as they could from the ships, he described the heavy weight of responsibility he felt. Obviously, the action was happening way too fast to count the number of men they were able to pull from danger. Many countless lives were saved from death that night.

How many people were rescued, you ask? He could not say, as that was not his focus at all. There was one man in particular who had slipped and fallen. In spite of the most intense, best efforts he could possibly give, my pastor shared in tremendous grief that he could not quite grasp his hand well enough to save him. The drowning man slipped away into the night and lost his life.

Not a pin drop could be heard through the audience as he described the severe anguish that tore into his soul about this single lost man. Indeed, he was sharing this that had happened forty years ago; yet the memories, and even the heartache, all remained so fresh and vivid. He later found out the name of the man, and remembered with piercing accuracy the date his life was lost in unreachably deep, dark waters. Yes, this man was only one life, and he was certainly no one famous or notoriously successful or important as far as this world's system recorded. Nevertheless, this one life mattered profoundly to the teenage boy who tried so hard to rescue him, but with hands too slippery to hold.[1]

Connecting this example of earthly experience to the heart of Father God for the lives He has personally created was the point of his sharing such a dramatic, true life story. Jesus, Who is a perfect image of the Father, giving us a picture of what God is like in everything He said and did on earth, gave the parable of the lost coin, the lost sheep, and the lost son in Luke 15.[2] We are so inclined by this world's system of math that we tend to count numbers in the masses, as higher statistics get our attention best—the more the better. God is the opposite. He cares and counts one-by-one. He is focused on the one lost, not the masses rescued. Just like my pastor was describing this painful story, even through the years, he has only been able to count that one man who perished, while having not the foggiest clue how many lives his crew may have saved that dark, frightening night.

Heaven throws a celebration party when just one lost soul comes Home to the heart of God through accepting Jesus as Lord and Savior! It is one life at a time that captures the careful attention of God. Does your life really matter? Absolutely!

In Luke 15, starting with the lost coin, everything in the house was turned upside down until it was found. Have you ever searched for something desperately important, and you made a mess trying to find it? Maybe you were running late and could not find your keys. It mattered not that you had other keys, maybe in a safe place, that belonged to your storage unit, your backyard shed, or other places. You only needed the one key that could start your car! That was the lost one, and that's the one you needed to find with utter determination and focus. So you rummage through all the papers on the desk, lifting things right and left, and leaving no rock unturned, so to speak, just to find that one important key that matters most to you. God certainly does not need to look for you; He knows exactly where you are. This is just an illustration of the lengths He will go for that one life He is determined to help and save; because only you can fulfill the unique, special purpose He gave *you*. It's not just about what you can "do," however. You are extremely important to Him, so He will stop at nothing to reach you just so He can show you His love, since you are the target of His affection.

Likewise, as a picture of what a Good Shepherd He is, He gives an illustration of a lost sheep. Although He has an entire fold already within His safe bounds where they are secured from harm, He is focused on the one that has strayed and is lost. So He leaves the ninety-nine and goes after that one! God counts by one! It is one life at a time that matters intensely to Him. One time, I took in a stray little dog who was roaming the streets. We bonded instantly, so he gratefully joined my other dogs who were also rescues. However, since my others were big, I had no idea there was a small gap in the back fence through which my new little one could escape and go exploring. In my heart, I knew he didn't want to leave his new happy home, but did I ever get upset when I discovered he was gone! No matter that my other big dogs were safe and happy; it was my wandering, lost one that I flew into action to find! I was desperately grateful to find him, as he had not gotten far at all, nor was he harmed by passing cars; but the beat of my heart was definitely in high pulse fashion until he was safely in my arms again. So it is with our Good Shepherd. He knows the potential dangers when we wander away from His covering of protection. If you have strayed from Him, let His loving arms bring you back to the home of His heart, where you will be safe and restored.

The man with the lost son is also a picture of how God numbers His own one by one, with each life mattering deeply to Him. That father in Luke 15 had a hole in his heart, as it were, as long as one of his sons was missing. It wasn't good enough that one was already home. He cared with great anguish about the lost one, no matter how much that particular son had ruined his life and spent his inheritance. Restoration of a life is always God's priority. When just one person returns to Him, there is unspeakable joy for the Father! Just look at the description Jesus gave of that earthly father celebrating the return of his lost boy. He threw a big party, sacrificed the best fatted calf for a feast, and put an expensive robe and sandals on his dirty feet. He even put a signet ring on his finger, symbolizing ownership of the most lasting covenant kind.

In fact, such strong meaning is portrayed by the ring detail. This was not only a restoration of his dignity—in spite of the wasted inheritance and financial loss, and the shame of a ruined life he bore; but it was a special seal of the father showing unconditional love and sonship that he belonged in that family no matter what. "Often considered the 'gentleman's ring,' the signet ring has been around since the days of the Old Testament, when it was used as a personal signature or symbol of family heritage. Typically it bore a family crest or another symbol representing an individual on its distinguishable flat bezel. A design was usually engraved (often in reverse) either directly into the metal of the ring or an inset gem, and then pressed into wax or clay to create the personal seal, or signature."[3] Do you think God would have used this detail in His Word for nothing? With a smile on my face, let me tell you, God loves details; nothing is by accident or coincidence with Him. If He illustrates this profound seal of a signet ring that the earthly father put on his son's finger as he returned home, how much more does He want to embrace your return home to His heart with His personal signature. You are offered a family heritage in Him that will last forever—a seal of your Father's unconditional love that you do matter greatly to Him, and that you do belong in His family.

So, with a resounding "yes" answer, without even having met you, I can assure you with absolute certainty that your life has tremendous value. You may be reading this from a prison cell, or you might have had an abortion yesterday. Maybe you were given up at birth for adoption, causing you to carry a weight of worthlessness and feeling unwanted all your life. No matter where you are, what you have done, or how you have been rejected or treated as trash, your life still does have immeasurable value in God's eyes! Hear it directly from the heart of God: "'For I know the plans I have for you,' declares the LORD, 'plans to prosper you and not to harm you, plans to give you hope and a future'" (Jeremiah 29:11 NIV).

David, who went from being a shepherd boy to a king, struggled relentlessly with cyclical bouts of depression and anxiety, but always found his way back to hope by lifting up his eyes to the greatness and faithfulness of God through worship. He cried out to God so many times when his soul was crushed to the core, and when King Saul was literally trying to kill him. One truth David held so firmly throughout all his trying times was that he had worth in His Father's eyes. This was what he used to encourage himself, and it was written in historical recordings so that we may do the same. Here is how one of his prayers sounded during an especially close bonding time he had alone with His Creator:

> "O LORD, you have examined my heart
> and know everything about me.
> You know when I sit down or stand up.
> You know my thoughts even when I'm far away.
> You see me when I travel
> and when I rest at home.
> You know everything I do.
> You know what I am going to say
> even before I say it, LORD.
> You go before me and follow me.
> You place your hand of blessing on my head.
> Such knowledge is too wonderful for me,

too great for me to understand!
I can never escape from your Spirit!
I can never get away from your presence!
If I go up to heaven, you are there;
if I go down to the grave, you are there.
If I ride the wings of the morning,
if I dwell by the farthest oceans,
even there your hand will guide me,
and your strength will support me.
I could ask the darkness to hide me
and the light around me to become night—
but even in darkness I cannot hide from you.
To you the night shines as bright as day.
Darkness and light are the same to you.
You made all the delicate, inner parts of my body
and knit me together in my mother's womb.
Thank you for making me so wonderfully complex!
Your workmanship is marvelous—how well I know it.
You watched me as I was being formed in utter seclusion,
as I was woven together in the dark of the womb.
You saw me before I was born.
Every day of my life was recorded in your book.
Every moment was laid out
before a single day had passed.
How precious are your thoughts about me, O God.
They cannot be numbered!
I can't even count them;
they outnumber the grains of sand!
And when I wake up,
you are still with me!
O God, if only you would destroy the wicked!
Get out of my life, you murderers!
They blaspheme you;

> your enemies misuse your name.
> O LORD, shouldn't I hate those who hate you?
> Shouldn't I despise those who oppose you?
> Yes, I hate them with total hatred,
> for your enemies are my enemies.
> Search me, O God, and know my heart;
> test me and know my anxious thoughts.
> Point out anything in me that offends you,
> and lead me along the path of everlasting life."
> (PSALM 139 NLT)

---

1 Feldschau, Pastor Randy. "The Power of One." Cathedral In The Pines, Beaumont, TX. July 9, 2017. Sermon.

2 Hebrews 1:3, John 5:19-21

3 Screws, Nic. "Everything You Need to Know About Wearing a Signet Ring—The millennia-old symbols of family and personal identity are experiencing a popular resurgence. But how should you wear yours?" Posted August 24, 2015, 10:43 AM, CDT. Bloomberg. www.bloomberg.com. https://www.bloomberg.com/news/articles/2015-08-24/everything-you-need-to-know-about-wearing-a-signet-ring Accessed May 18, 2018.

THE DEAD CAN'T THINK AHEAD

You are God's beloved one. Your life is precious and valuable to Him. Therefore, to live or to die is your hardest, most important decision at this time. You may disagree, thinking that it is the pressuring decision to have an abortion or not, for example; or some other heavy decision consuming your focus. However, no matter the extreme importance and validity those pressing factors may have, the truth is that your choice for life or death is where your decision must begin as a necessary precedence for any other matter. For instance, if you are contemplating suicide as a seemingly easier alternative than birthing or aborting your child, know that your choice to live affects not just two lives—your baby's and your own, but your choice impacts countless generations to come.

The consequences are weighty and everlasting. Although you may be blinded to it right now by the endless sea of tears and pain in your darkest hours, your prized destiny is at stake. As you read through some promptings for pondering, be assured that you are not alone in this, no matter how severe the pain is within your broken heart and dead-end feelings. One is standing by ready to help and bring comfort when you might least expect it. My prayer is that you will begin to feel the presence of the Lord drawing close to you as you read this book. He is waiting on your request for Him, because He is never pushy, demanding, or controlling. He is just Love in its purest form;

and that will include comforting and helping you if and when you are ready to receive His help, grace, and mercy. Such a Love is available to all who call upon His Name—Jesus. You will even find incredible healing just to speak His name out loud, no matter how faint the whispering sound.

Have you been wrestling with this ambivalence over time? Is it your Plan B exit strategy that you gives you relief just to know it's there as an option in your mind for the day you just can't go on? Make it easier on yourself, ironically, by removing that option from your mind altogether. That is precisely where the enemy takes advantage of you. His opened door is that back-up plan in your mind, as doubt and unbelief give him entrance and full access to torment you about it, keeping you unstable. He will push and keep on pushing you until you give in, which is exactly what he wants. His aim is always to steal, kill, and destroy. In James 1:8, the Word says that this double-mindedness makes you unstable in all your ways. So do yourself a great favor by resolving that the back-up plan to end your life is no longer there. As you let the peace of Christ rule as umpire in your mind, having all doubts removed, the torment of wavering and instability will be removed.[1] The rest of this book is dedicated to helping you walk out this resolve, but it begins with this big step of removing that exit strategy you're holding in the back of your mind as pseudo peace. David Jeremiah said, "If you can remember, when in a battle, that the victory is already won, then you can fight with confidence…'Keep Calm and Carry On.'"[2]

Making the decision to live can prove to be a special pivotal turning point in your life's course and direction. God says, "…I have set before you life and death, blessings and cursings. Now choose life, so that you and your children may live" (Deuteronomy 30:19 NIV). Why would the same God Who gives us free will pose a question to us and then immediately supply the answer Himself? Perhaps it's because He knows what profound consequences either choice would have, and loves us so much that He wants to spare us the agony of curses that choosing death would have. He, as the eternal God—the Alpha and Omega—knows the beginning from the end. Psalm 139:16 says that all our days were numbered and took shape before even one of them came to pass. Our minds, ways, and thoughts are terribly finite, but God's are just the opposite: infinite, so much higher than ours, stretching from one end of the globe to the other in His grand panoramic view, with plans He established long before we were created.

It is still our choice to make, but the loving heartbeat of the Father, as our Creator, knows what all He has planned for us if we will take the initiative in choosing life. Jeremiah 29:11 speaks of God's future plans. They are hope and peace in our final outcome, not of harm. This is not to be confused with the myth of a problem-free life implied for a Christian. For Jesus Himself said in John 16:33, "In this life, you will have trouble; but take heart, I have overcome the world." In many other places throughout Scripture, suffering is not only part of life; it is a vehicle for our spiritual growth, our emotional and mental integrity, our character development, and a testing of our faith, to name a few.[3]

We can expect that our character development, growth, process of sanctification, and being chastised by the Lord are all parts of our walk with the Lord. We go through fires of affliction, refinement, and purification so that our faith and character can deepen and strengthen, ultimately in developing a sweeter intimacy with Jesus, Who loves us far too much to leave us the way we are when we first come to Him! This is hope, however, not doom! It can be our joy, in other words, to share in the sufferings of Christ; for it is a powerful realization to be considered worthy to suffer for His sake. The apostles Paul and Peter both testified to this in their own lives. Their love and devotion for Jesus was so life-changing and passionate that they truly considered it an honor to be chosen to share in the sufferings of Christ, as a proof and sign of His ownership of them; and we can adopt the same attitude, even despite what is causing this debilitating depression and sorrow of heart. Again, drawing from Jeremiah 29:11, it is not that we are spared from trouble along the journey; it is that hope and peace are promised in our "final outcome," regardless of what our narrow minds see from day to day.

This is precisely why it is so vitally important to press through this death-gripping temptation of suicide. You would be deliberately aborting all those plans and the final outcome God has planned for you personally, as the apple of His eye.[4] You are at a defining crossroads with this decision. What you choose will have consequences either way. If you will receive it into your heart how much God loves you and yearns to hold you very close these days as you walk through your valley of the shadow of death, you will find the courage needed to live. We cannot manufacture this on our own, especially when pain has so blinded and crippled us, including our own sense of bravery to face life in such a broken state. In fact, in another chapter, we will explore how futile our own strength really is in carrying out even our best intentions. For now, simply know and rest in the fact that God will absolutely help you with the smallest details of your situation, to the severely overwhelming extremes of it as well, never expecting you to handle it all alone. He has the strength we need. It has to come from Him, if it is to come at all. This mountain you are facing can and will be removed; but it is "Not by might, nor by power, but by My Spirit, says the Lord of hosts" (Zechariah 4:6 ESV).

It takes a much stronger person to make the decision under this kind of painful pressure to live. Although this particular choice carries the weight of eternity, think of other significant, albeit lesser, decisions you have made in the past in which you may even feel gratitude for having made the decision you did at that time. This foreshadows a day in which you will retrospectively look back to this season of your life in a similar thankful, awestruck and humbled way. At that time, when the painful dense fog of current times has lifted, imagine the depth of gratitude and clarity of thought you will have, as a means of reaching for hope and strength "now." After all, we need to stay ever mindful of how faithful God has been in seeing us through difficult, tight spots, and painful experiences of the past, while recalling that He is the same yesterday, today, and forever.[5] The Psalmist David did this regularly as he encouraged himself in the Lord during his downcast times. When has God ever failed? When has He never been enough? Invariably, we find ourselves in the presence of a faithful God, no matter how dark and bleak circumstances may appear. In fact, in Hebrews, it says that Jesus is our steadfast Hope, as an Anchor for the soul.[6]

However, this retrospective view can work in the opposite direction also. Can you recall decisions that you made poorly and wish you could go back and change, but it was too late? Even now, as you recall it, you no doubt reel in remorse and regret. Maybe this certain pain is why you're tempted with suicide in the first place. If only you could go back to undo and redo—but it is too late. Consider this: from an eternal perspective, those already on the other side simply have no option to undo or redo a single thing. They cannot say a single word to anyone, or attempt to make amends for anything that might have brought healing to all involved. Their story has been permanently inked, sealed, and ended as history now. Because the dead can no longer think ahead, regrets linger as the stench of all that is left. Yet we who remain have the incredible gift (whether it feels like a gift or not) to create in present tense that which will become our history later. As long as we still have breath and life, we have the power to decide, say, and act upon certain convictions that can change our course for the better. If it was possible, surely the most powerful regret of all would be to look back—once we are on the other side—and wish that we had given it a little more time, a little more patience to wait upon God to help and come through in some creatively planned way, a little more grace given to others and ourselves for having failed; or a little more time given to whatever else the driving force is that tempts us so much with a dead-end, "no way out" type of feeling.

In conclusion, this most important decision of yours is only made possible when you trust God to help you choose life one day at a time. You don't have to slay all your giants in one day, or conquer your entire future in this moment. He only asks you to choose life in this one day that He has given you. It really is a gift, whether it feels like it or not. Listen to how much your life truly matters. "You made all the delicate, inner parts of my body and knit them together in my mother's womb. Thank You for making me so wonderfully complex! It is amazing to think about. Your workmanship is marvelous—and how well I know it. You were there while I was being formed in utter seclusion! You saw me before I was born and scheduled each day of my life before I began to breathe. Every day was recorded in Your book! How precious it is, Lord, to realize that you are thinking about me constantly! I can't even count how many times a day Your thoughts turn toward me. And when I waken in the morning, You are still thinking of me!" (Psalm 139:13-18 TLB)

Although you may start to shift into the decisive choice to live as being the critically most important decision, you still might wonder, "How?" Glad you asked! Remember, Jesus promised He would not leave us comfortless or as orphans (implying helpless, without protection or provision, and alone); but that we will be equipped with the most powerful Companion as our Helper, Advocate, Intercessor, Comforter, Counselor, Strengthener, and Standby.[7] These are all the names given to His Holy Spirit—our guarantee that we are never, ever alone. In His empowering help and strength, our "how?" question is always answered.

Even in such a life-or-death decision as this is, with the pressure of temptation making an end to the pain all too appealing, realize that because you are deeply valuable to God, He isn't even asking you to make this leap of a choice alone. Picture Him reaching His nail-scarred hands of help to you in creative ways even now. Begin to look for Him in this, and you will find Him. The help and presence of Holy Spirit is ready to be activated within you, as He is yearning to give you a newfound sense of hope and promise for a brighter future—even beginning this moment!

---

1 Colossians 3:15

2 Jeremiah, David. *Living With Confidence in a Chaotic World: What on Earth Should We Do Now?* Nashville, TN: Thomas Nelson, 2016.

3 Psalm 34:19; 119:71
 Romans 5:3-4; 8:18, 35-39
 II Corinthians 1:3-4-10; 4:8-10,17
 James 1:2-4,12
 I Peter 1:6-9; 3:14; 4:12-13; 5:10
 Revelation 21:4-7

4 Psalm 17:8

5 Hebrews 13:8

6 Hebrews 6:19

7 John 14:15-27 AMP

PEACE IS POSSIBLE

Peace comes at a Price. We do not have to pay it, however! Jesus was literally punished (in our places, instead of us) so that we could have peace. This is a costly gift so graciously offered to us for free, simply for the self-surrender and humility in accepting it. Let's not ignore or waste it! Rather, be ever so moved by gratitude to embrace it, receive it, and live fully in it. Panic may rise; but peace can fall in its place as a blanket or covering, extinguishing the fiery darts of the enemy on every side. Jesus admonished us not to "let ourselves" be agitated, troubled, disturbed, or afraid. Not only does God remind us 365 times throughout His Word not to be afraid (one for every day of the year), but in John 14, Jesus is talking about the promised Holy Spirit Who will come as our personal Comforter. He gives us a gift of internal, lasting peace through not only the brutal punishment He took upon Himself on the cross in that one event at Calvary; but now, through an eternally lasting, daily relationship, we can have His own Spirit indwelling us as a means of living in this very real peace instead of giving way to panic, anxiety, and fear.

I personally struggled with anxiety, including debilitating panic attacks and insomnia for many years. In fact, the years-long battle I had with anorexia cycled around anxiety, as a continual quest for peace; only to realize time after defeating time that it was a false peace at best. A state of starvation had a calming effect on me, until something would trigger anxiety all over again. Peace never lasted when it was my own established definition of it, such as thorough exhaustion after abusive overexertion in exercise or some other physical labor that naturally exceeded my own strength. If you experience the madness of drivenness, excessive work, and addictions all in attempts to find peace, you know precisely the futility and frustration I'm describing by the pseudo peace that never lasts, and hardly delivers. But Jesus gives us hope in telling us that the kind of peace He gives isn't like the kind the world gives. His version of peace is not only authentic, which He says we can have even in the midst of chaotic circumstances, since it's the kind that surpasses our understanding; but coming from Him as the source makes it an everlasting kind. Thus, we cannot lose it from day to day, even when life hurls its ugliest blows and volatility surrounds us.

We find a Kingdom key to this stability of lasting peace in Isaiah 26:3-4 (AMP), "You will guard him and keep him in perfect and constant peace whose mind [both its inclination and its character] is stayed on You, because he commits himself to You, leans on You, and hopes confidently in You. So trust in the Lord (commit yourself to Him, lean on Him, hope confidently in Him) forever; for the Lord God is an everlasting Rock [the Rock of Ages]." The key is to keep our minds on Jesus, off ourselves and our problems.

From my own journey, I discovered another very specific aspect of just how healing and possible this peace truly is for us, simply for the receiving it. Did you know that God specifically invites and welcomes those who are miserable with the consequences of sin to experience His special gift of peace? In this chapter will be shared how I stumbled upon this specific revelation, what all it unfolded for my freedom, and how it can do the same for you. Because self-condemnation was a pit that daily swallowed me up for many years, this amazing discovery brought so much healing, joy, and liberty to my life that overwhelms me with passion to share, so that others in the same bondage and suffering can also be liberated unto joy!

If you take time to explore and devour the book of Hebrews for all its worth, you'll find that it's a book dripping rich with hope. It can touch those so broken and crushed beneath the yoke of slavery and bondage in trying so hard to earn their own way of salvation, peace, or a sense of goodness; yet who are daily experiencing the frustration and hopelessness of falling short of perfection, all because it's law-driven. In other words, even in modern day, we tend to live out Old Covenant ways of living, such as trying to pay for our guilt, shame, and sin by way of self-atonement. This looks differently among people; but its core is the same in that we are striving in our own efforts to be good enough—ultimately to attain peace. This will never work! In fact, it's even detestable to God; because our own righteousness is like filthy rags to Him. However, in the precious bloodshed of Jesus, a Better Way of living was opened up to us, inviting us to experience and receive an unprecedented hope. We find that what the law could never accomplish for us, since we could never keep it flawlessly, we get introduced to the New Covenant by way of Jesus' atonement for us—which all of a sudden makes peace, hope, grace, freedom, and joy absolutely possible for a change! We are literally invited to enter into the rest of God. That is, we are offered a hope beyond all our striving (since it never amounted to being enough anyway); and instead are given the chance to appropriate all that Jesus did for us as our means of being not only acceptable to God, but an accessibility to be intimately close to Him as our Father, even bold before Him as our God. Having peace with God is the only way we can be at peace with ourselves.

Just as the blood of bulls and goats was never sufficient back in the day when animal sacrifices were made, so our own efforts of self-atonement are never enough either, be they excessive drivenness in work, or abusing our bodies to achieve some peaceful effect, or trying to be good enough by other self-atoning efforts. Through Jesus alone, all our debts have been paid in full. Our sin penalty has been cancelled! Jesus took the punishment for our peace upon Himself. He was beaten and brutally abused, tortured, and killed, all so that He could declare, "It Is Finished!" (John 19:30). All the punishment we deserve was absorbed by our loving Jesus in His own body for us. So these profound words, "It is finished!" still echo from His heart to us today from His position of power at God's right hand. Everything He suffered and endured for us is now ours. That is, we can now have right standing with God, through the robe of righteousness that Jesus puts on us. There are deep Kingdom secrets and treasures that the book of Hebrews opens to us about the New Covenant and all that Jesus accomplished for us. Entering into His rest, therefore, is one of the incredible prizes of His presence that is found as we plunge ourselves into the truths offered here. This becomes the entrance gate, as it were, to our lasting peace.

As an infinitely loving, merciful Father would thrill at speaking in His own Word, "Now may the God of peace [the source of serenity and spiritual well-being] who brought up from the dead our Lord Jesus, the great Shepherd of the sheep, through the blood that sealed and ratified the eternal covenant, equip you with every good thing to carry out His will and strengthen you [making you complete and perfect as you ought to be], accomplishing in us that which is pleasing in His sight, through Jesus Christ, to whom be the glory forever and ever. Amen" (Hebrews 13:20-21 AMP).

Prepare to be amazed! Researching word origins here, "peace" in the above verse is referring to the certain peace that God gives to those who are miserable with sin's consequences! If you have lived under this burden, even to the point of despair as I was, be encouraged! God addresses us specifically with mercy from it all! The root word is *eirene*. In Hebrew, this means "peace, rest, in contrast with strife; denoting the absence or end of strife. *Eirene* denotes a state of untroubled, undisturbed, well-being. When contrasted with strife, such a state of peace is the object of divine promise and is brought about by God's mercy."[1] It is a special state of peace specifically defined as "granting deliverance and freedom from all the distresses that are experienced as a result of sin. Used together with *eleos*, it refers to mercy for the consequences of sin, and also with *charis*, grace, which affects the character of the person. Peace as a Messianic blessing is that state brought about by the grace and loving mind of God wherein the derangement and distress of life caused by sin are removed. Hence the message of salvation is called the Gospel of peace."[2] "This is the message God sent to the people of Israel, telling the good news of peace through Jesus Christ, Who is Lord of all" (Acts 10:36).

"It is called the peace of God...the result only of accomplished reconciliation, referring to the new relationship between man and God brought about by the atonement."[3] It is synonymous with *asphaleia*, meaning security.[4] "Do not be anxious about anything, but in everything by prayer and petition, with thanksgiving, present your requests to God. And the peace of God, which transcends all understanding, will guard your hearts and your minds in Christ Jesus" (Philippians 4:7). "Since we have now been justified by His blood, how much more shall we be saved from God's wrath through Him! For if, when we were God's enemies, we were reconciled to Him through the death of His Son, how much more, having been reconciled, shall we be saved through His life! Not only is this so, but we also rejoice in God through our Lord Jesus Christ, through Whom we have now received reconciliation" (Romans 5:9-11).

If you do not yet know Jesus personally as your Lord and Savior, now would be a great time to receive Him so that you can indeed find this peace you are so desperately needing and seeking. At the back of this book, you will find a Prayer for Salvation as a guide to help you with this incredibly life-changing decision.

> "When someone becomes a Christian, he becomes a brand new person inside. He is not the same anymore. A new life has begun! All these things are from God Who brought us back to Himself through what Christ Jesus did.
>
> And God has given us the privilege of urging everyone to come into His favor and be reconciled to Him. For God was in Christ,

restoring the world to Himself, no longer counting men's sins against them but blotting them out.

This is the wonderful message He has given us to tell others. We are Christ's ambassadors. God is using us to speak to you: we beg you as though Christ Himself were here pleading with you, receive the love He offers you—be reconciled to God.

For God took the sinless Christ and poured into Him our sins. Then, in exchange, He poured God's goodness into us!" (II Corinthians 5:17-21 TLB)

Wait, there is more! We get showered by another gift of liberating truth, in that *He* is the One Who does the work of peace and completion in us and for us![5] One of the beautiful names of God is *Jehovah Shalom*, the Lord our Peace. *Shalom* is a Hebrew word meaning wholeness, completion—nothing broken, nothing missing. This is part of God's nature; thus He wants to bless your life with *shalom*.

Again, we are delivered from all our own efforts of trying to attain a temporal peace. We are simply clothed with such a love here that the Spirit of God specifically reaches out with infinite mercy and grace to those burdened by the miseries that sin's consequences have produced. Not only has Jesus' atonement accomplished our forgiveness and right standing with God, but as for the rest of the journey, we can have perfect peace in ceasing all striving; because He is the One Who promises to complete the work He wants to see in us! He invites our utter dependency on Him; and ironically, this is precisely where and how we experience His peace—finally!

Make no mistake, this peace *is* definitely the lasting kind! What is more, this peace *is* most certainly possible. That is what echoed from the dark sky on the day that the Spotless Lamb of God hung on a cruel cross instead of us and shouted in His last breath: "It is Finished!" Yes, peace of *His* kind is available, simply for the believing, receiving, and humbly entering into this amazing rest of God from all our laboring and self-payment attempts!

In closing, I want to share the peace-giving words that Jesus has spoken directly. Drink of this deeply into your heart, mind, and soul to the fullest measure. "Peace I leave with you; My perfect peace I give to you; not as the world gives do I give to you. Do not let your heart be troubled, nor let it be afraid. Let My perfect peace calm you in every circumstance and give you courage and strength for every challenge" (John 14:27 AMP).

1, 2, 3, 4 Zodhiates, Spiros. *Hebrew-Greek Key Word Study Bible King James Version.* "Lexical Aids to the New Testament." Revised Edition. Chattanooga, TN: AMG Publishers, 1991.

5 Hebrews 13:21 AMP

THE MASTERMIND OF EVIL

A battle is being waged over our minds everyday. Whereas cold-blooded murder, theft, or violent destruction of people and property manifest in ways that are easily visible in the physical realm, the war taking place in your mind is seemingly invisible, yet far more dangerous. Not only is it where those other overt criminal acts originate, but our very souls are at stake. We hear people joking about devils and hell, but nothing is funny about it. Hell is a very real place, and the devil is not just playing games in a Halloween costume; he is real. Satan was banned from heaven when he coveted the place and praise of God. Ever since he was thrust out of heaven, he has been on an evil rage to take every soul with him to hell that he can lure. His strategy is far from blatant; it is subtle and sly, being the master of deception that he is.

His primary goal is not only to steal, kill, and destroy your life; it is to get you to come in agreement with him. This way, he wins. All his strategies are much easier once he has your mind engaged and agreeing with the lies he's whispering into your head day and night. You think it's your own thoughts, but that's not true. We are either listening to our Creator speaking truth and Life, or our enemy speaking lies and death. There is no neutral ground. Even Christians who have been walking with Jesus a long time still continue to struggle with this type of warfare. You are not alone! No condemnation is in this book whatsoever. In fact, this is just to expose the darkness by letting you know it's not you! If you're feeling like there must be something wrong with you that you're struggling with suicide temptation so severely, take heart; it's not the case. You are being targeted by the enemy of your very soul, yet in his crafty scheme, he's putting all the shame and condemnation on you that you're somehow dark and different. Obviously, he's using that to drive you further to suicide. Don't let him. He is a liar.

Have you ever had one of those days, or perhaps a stretch of weeks, where you were especially low and kept blurting out, "I am so hopeless," "I hate my life," or "I'm going to kill myself"? It may have been muttered under your breath, or out loud in exasperation or rage; or it may have even been said within a conversation to someone else. If so, think about what happened in the atmosphere immediately following your words. Did it not become all the darker, more hopeless, and you began to think of how to carry out your plan? There is a reason for this, and I'll share from personal experience how I discovered it.

I was guilty of doing this quite often in my struggles with suicide temptation. Life had just become too painful at times, so my insides were absolutely screaming for relief. Addictions, the enemy's favorite game, had my throat and no longer offered a salve for my soul. Raw, trapped, and wounded, I would sob uncontrollably, sighing these very phrases; but every time I did, I noticed how much more severe the temptation became, and how the darkness intensified. I also began to realize how much the presence of God seemed to lift dramatically. His gentle conviction power was definitely at work; as you must know, Jesus is fighting for us in this war, every bit as much as the enemy is fighting *against* us!

What Jesus finally penetrated my heart to understand was that I was literally grieving His Holy Spirit in a deep way, because I was defying, rebelling, and opposing the same Spirit of God Who initially breathed life into me at birth. Because He is such a Gentleman, He only comes where He is invited. By my words, even though sometimes I thought I was "praying" by saying, "God, I'm just so hopeless. I beg You to let me die," it was actually like I was rejecting Him, His presence, His life, and all the truth of His Word. To say I was praying amiss would be an understatement. In the famous "love chapter," we find that "love is patient," whereas suicide temptation is pressing, demanding, and pushing—"I want out of this pain *now*!" "Love does not delight in evil but rejoices with the truth,…it always trusts, *always hopes*, always perseveres."[1] Many years ago, I heard a pastor challenge us to read I Corinthians 13 and put the name of Jesus everywhere that it says the word, "love." You will discover His character this way. Then, read it again putting your own name in place of the word, "love." This is our aim of how to live. Therefore, when I was uttering the abovementioned hopeless phrases, you can see how grieved the Spirit of God was. I was defiantly expressing all the opposites: "I hate my life, I am hopeless, I want out of my pain *now*!" No wonder I sensed the presence of God lift; I was rejecting Him and all the truth that embodies His love.

On the other hand, the enemy relished and feasted on my hopeless mutterings. He celebrated that I was coming into agreement with him, which invited all the more of his dark, hopeless, evil presence. Do you see how this works? I was surrendering ground to the mastermind of evil, opening wide a door for him to access even more of me, which is why I experienced an intensified darkness, hopelessness, and stronger force of suicide temptation by coming into agreement with all the lies he had been pushing me to believe. Do we easily recognize they are lies at the time? Of course not! Remember, he is a master artist at deception. The hopeful news is, however, when you immerse yourself in God's truth, and "live in the Light as He is in the Light,"[2] it does get much easier to discern when you are being fed his lies.

The man in the Bible most famously known for his suffering, Job, was taunted and tempted by his wife who had reached her satiation point with all the losses and pain, thus decisively had given up on life when she said to him, "Curse God and die." At this, hell clapped in great applause; for it was precisely the achieved goal Satan had been targeting all along. Since God had made the one stipulation that Satan could not end Job's physical life, all he [Satan] had to do was get Job to so vehemently give up on God as to take his own life. Far easier for the culprit of such evil to hide conveniently behind the disguise that he did "nothing" to Job's life, except obviously wear down his strength, steal his joy, silence his praise, cloud his view, and twist his understanding of God's nearness.

Imagine the worst evil that you possibly can. Perhaps it is something that has happened to you personally, or a horrible atrocity to a loved one; or maybe a more detached awareness of some other situation that has given you the indelible impression of severe evil. Even the coronavirus global pandemic with all its cruel effects, including the loss of many lives and disastrous economic disruptions serve as great examples.

With this vividly in your mind, realize that Satan was the mastermind behind it; he literally was the creator, instigator, and perpetrator of it as the source. Once you see that there is a mean face—and know whose it is—behind this outrageous evil, know that this same face is exactly who will get the glory and credit for your suicide attempt. He will be the only one, in fact, not hurt by your choice, but rather celebratory at his great accomplishment of victory in killing you by your own hands, not even having to use his own to win his triumph.

Alternatively, there is a Redeemer Who is not pushy, and will not coerce you into any action you may later regret. He knew your name before you were born. He was there as the breath of God was giving you the first breath of life; and He was there when you uttered your first cry as a newborn thrust from that safe place into this great unknown. However, it was not unknown to Him. He had a covenant to keep with you that was put into place thousands of generations ago. It was a covenant of peace and completion, even when your world would fall apart to the point of your feeling suicidal.

God says this covenant promise in such a beautiful way. "For this is like the days of Noah to Me; as I swore that the waters of Noah should no more go over the earth, so have I sworn that I will not be angry with you or rebuke you. For though the mountains should depart and the hills be shaken or removed, yet My love and kindness shall not depart from you, nor shall My covenant of peace and completeness be removed, says the Lord, Who has compassion on you" (Isaiah 54:9-10 AMP).

Taking a zoomed-in view of who God was talking to first when He said this was His beloved people of Israel. We are now included in this promise, which is later discussed in this book; but for now, I want to illustrate a point for you. Mike Evans and Curt Landry are two great examples of ministry leaders known worldwide for their outreaches and ongoing support for Jewish people. Ironically, both men were nearly aborted at birth. This is indeed part of their testimonies that their mothers opted against having an abortion after all. Consider what would have happened had these men been aborted at birth. Their lives have been mightily used of God to bring hope to countless Jews, Holocaust survivors, Israel Defense Forces soldiers, Safe Houses in Israel for youth who would otherwise be homeless, and the outreaches continue of all they are doing to this day. They have been an integral part of God's covenant of peace and completion being fulfilled! The enemy had plans to stop this by hindering their birth. God's plans, ways, thoughts, and purposes are higher every time.

That same covenant of peace and completion is a song He sings over your life as well. Yes, the enemy is doing all he can to abort that progress in your life, but he only wins if you let him. Jesus said that in this world, we would definitely have trouble; but He told us to take heart, and to be of good cheer, because He has overcome the world.[3] Take sides with Jesus, not your enemy who is intent on destroying you. There is not one thing you have ever done, or ever could do, to make Jesus stop loving you. He already paid the price to set you free; nothing can undo that famous, costly Bloodshed that was actually for you! This is the face of purest love and grace that would be most honored if you chose to lay down your self-inflicted weapon of suicide.

Love personified in the Man named Jesus is not just about receiving the glory though. He is longing to help you cross over that death-line into His abundant life, eager and ready to help you every step of the way. The evil minded one stalking and taunting you into the defeat of suicide, which would be the only ultimate, irreversible failure, would only be throwing you away after his victory of your death. The choice is clear, but you must be the one to make it.

> "For we are not wrestling with flesh and blood [contending only with physical opponents], but against the despotisms, against the powers, against [the master spirits who are the world rulers of this present darkness, against the spirit forces of wickedness in the heavenly (supernatural) sphere" (Ephesians 6:12 AMPC).

> "For though we walk (live) in the flesh, we are not carrying on our warfare according to the flesh and using mere human weapons. For the weapons of our warfare are not physical [weapons of flesh and blood], but they are mighty before God for the overthrow and destruction of strongholds" (II Corinthians 10:3-4 AMPC).

---

1 I Corinthians 13:4a,6

2 I John 1:7

3 John 16:33

LIFE AFTER FAILURE

Have you experienced the pain of failure? Is this the pounding cause of suicide temptation hammering your mind into a black hole of despair? Have you been terminated from a job or experienced profound financial loss? Perhaps a failed marriage has broken your heart seemingly beyond repair. Have you made yourself vulnerable in starting a new business or ministry, only for it to crumble and come to nothing? Has the chaos of current times left you reeling, shutting down your dreams, forcing you to start all over—perhaps in a new job or location due to forced evacuations after fires or floods? Maybe there is just a general sense of failure that plagues you in a persistent way, as if you are prone to failure no matter what you attempt. Please hear this most important truth: the only way to fail is to give up completely.

No one on this earth has escaped the reality of failure. To varying degrees, we have all failed in some way, simply because we are all imperfect human beings. Although your feelings of failure may have validity, our stories cannot be compared or measured as inferior or superior to others' experiences. Sometimes it does help to see beyond our own lives with grander perspective, however.

Here again, I write with overflowing empathy and compassion, as my words are drenched in personal experience of having walked through the pain of failure—more than once, in more ways than one! I understand firsthand the sense of loss and devastation that comes with the hurting sting of failure. The place of ruin and being faced with the need to start all over is where I have been myself, so I truly feel your pain if this is where you are. Even the agony of humiliation that can result from failure is not setting you apart as much as you might feel it is. If we can just be real and honest with each other, pride does take a harsh beating when we fail—however public and largely known our failures are. The heartache is no less intense, however, when our failures are only known by us in a private, acutely personal way.

An all-important fact for us to remember is that failure does not define who we are. For example, it may appear as a failure to experience job loss; but this may have simply occurred as a company downsizing and having no choice but to cut even the best employees. You may have failed an extra challenging class in college, but that still does not make you a failure. We tend to internalize failure as an identity—thinking of ourselves as failures when success is not achieved, goals aren't met, or when our hopes and dreams are dashed and broken, whether our fault or not. Yet this is a tragic mistake, because no matter the cause of having fallen short, our identity (for those who believe in Jesus and have received Him as Savior) is as stable as He is Himself, the Rock! It is critical that we not think of ourselves as failures. Why? Proverbs 23:7 says, as a man "thinks in his heart, so is he." Therefore, my friend, please be encouraged to know that nothing you have experienced has the power to make you a failure except your own thoughts! Your identity in Christ is unshaken and secured against failure defining who you are. So don't let your thoughts wage such a tormenting war convincing you that you are a failure. You are not!

If we have failed by committing some sin that seems unpardonable by even Christian people, it can be especially hard to forgive ourselves and move forward. The only sin that cannot be forgiven is blasphemy of the Holy Spirit. On this note, I have heard it said that if we are exceedingly concerned that we have crossed this line, we most assuredly haven't! That's because we would have lost all tenderness of heart altogether due to a stony, cold, indifference of heart towards Him.

In other words, if you are feeling deeply concerned with these very words, take heart, He is still wooing and drawing you, which would not be the case had you blatantly blasphemed against the Holy Spirit, utterly doubting and disbelieving Him. Therefore, please know that God has open arms of forgiveness for you no matter what you've done.

In fact, Jesus already made atonement on the cross; so He forgave you even before you committed any sin. Romans 5:8 says, "But God demonstrates His own love for us in that while we were *still* sinners, Christ died for us" (emphasis mine). Paraphrasing the next verse, it would have been easier, admirable, or more natural for Him to have died for someone who was noble and flawless; yet that's not what happened at all! It was while we were neck deep in our filthy shame, sin, and ruin that He stepped into the scene, took our punishments upon Himself, so that we would be spared of having to endure it ourselves. We honor this tremendous sacrifice He made when we humble ourselves before Him asking to receive that gracious gift of forgiveness which He made possible at Calvary. It blesses Him immensely for us to receive His forgiveness, and in turn, forgive ourselves. All the more honoring to Him it is, therefore, when we drop it and let it go.

Have you ever tried to give a gift to someone who refused and rejected it? How did you feel? All you wanted was for that person to receive with great joy what you were giving, right? So it is with Jesus. All the tormenting agony He suffered at the Cross was to cancel our failures, to enable forgiveness of ourselves, just as much as it was to enable us to forgive others. Receive it! That's what He wants you to do with overwhelming joy and relief!

By far, letting myself off the hook, so to speak, has been my most challenging part. I lived under such a cruel taskmaster of my own mindset that my behaviors were self-punishing, self-condemning, and driven by self-hatred. It required lots of effort and prayer to reprogram my mind to live in the light of God's forgiveness and grace as opposed to my perpetual self-punitive ways. The Word talks about renewing one's mind, being washed by the water of the Word, thereby having a fresh mental and spiritual attitude.[1] You would be amazed to find the theme of redemption running throughout the entire Bible. God's hallmark of character is mercy-driven, grace-given second chances. He never gives up on people! That is, unless they give up on Him and themselves by committing suicide, like Judas Iscariot did.

Even Rahab, a prostitute in the Old Testament was given the promised gift of redemption in that not only was her family spared from destruction that the rest of the city residents incurred; but God's love was so unconditional and forgiving that she was actually an integral part of the lineage of Jesus the Messiah! See, no one is disqualified when God has a redeeming plan and people yield themselves to it. Your past is always redeemable in God's eyes, because He is a forward focused Savior. You are not just saved from your past mistakes and failures; you are redeemed for reasons forthcoming, as God has great plans for your future!

Of course, one of the best examples of what God can do in redeeming failure is the Apostle Peter. Remember how miserably he failed, even in doing the very thing he stated with such confidence and certainty he would specifically *not* do? Jesus knew perfectly ahead of time that his bold declaration of not denying Him would turn into not just one failure, but multiplied by three. Peter meant well and had the best intentions, until he found out how weak he really was in the heat of the moment. He indeed "wept bitterly" at his infamous failure.[2] Even so, with the foreknowledge of how sorely Peter would blow it, Jesus had already boldly and full of grace told him that He would be praying for him—that his faith would not fail; and when he has turned, to strengthen his brothers. Surely enough, this is exactly what happened. Peter so thoroughly turned in repentance and humility; and not so long thereafter, thousands experienced the fullness of God's power and glory at Pentecost as a result of Peter's ministry. This is the Lord's heart for you as well. He is constantly praying for you at the right hand of the Father. He is not taken by surprise when you fail. Rather, like with Peter, He has an incredible plan to redeem that failure, such that you can turn and help others.

There is a special story in the Word that describes a man who nearly killed himself for fear of losing his job. It was the jailer who was in charge of keeping Paul and Silas locked behind bars. The story holds miraculous significance in how God in His sovereignty set them free, as He sent a violent earthquake that shook the very foundation of the prison that was holding them captive. This is a lesson all its own! What brought their freedom, by this earth-shaking phenomenon, was their praise and worship behind bars. However, the jailer grew so afraid that he turned his sword towards himself, no doubt convinced that he had failed at his job of keeping them locked up. Yet Paul and Silas yelled for him not to be afraid, that they were still there! In fact, they declared it was an opportunity for his salvation![3] Obviously, the jailer's attention was captured that two prisoners were still hanging around, let alone caring about him as their prison guard, even though their prison door broke loose such that they could have easily escaped. Therefore, all he could say was that he wanted what they had—even joy in prison! He cried out for salvation right then and there, as suicide was not his only way out at all! In God's eyes, he by no means failed on the job; he was offered great hope of eternal life. See how creative God is in turning crisis moments of near-suicide into amazing redemption stories?

As already stated, although comparisons are generally wise to avoid, we do find ourselves desperate to dig for hope and encouragement during times of failure as we reach for strength to rise from the ashes and begin again. Not only in the Word do we find these stories of hope and redemption, but even more recent history is full of people who profoundly failed—even repeatedly—but got back up to live again.

When is the last time you priced a Dyson vacuum cleaner? This is not a trick question! They easily sell for upwards of $400, but Sir James Dyson had over five thousand failed attempts before he actually succeeded with his four and a half billion enterprise.[4] If Walt Disney had given up due to failure, none of us would have nostalgic memories of all he created that we enjoyed as children, and which has enthralled every generation since. However, he had an editor tell him that he "lacked imagination and had no good ideas."[5] Walt Disney quotes, "I think it's important to have a good hard failure when you're young... Because it makes you kind of aware of what can happen to you. Because of it I've never had any fear in my whole life when we've been near collapse and all of that. I've never been afraid."[6] Thomas Edison was dealt the harsh blow of hearing such words by his teachers that he was "too stupid to learn anything."[7] If you're reading this by an electric lamp, you are not thinking of his failures at all, but rather enjoying one of his many successes! Albert Einstein did not start speaking until age four and didn't start reading until age seven; but he later won a Nobel Prize and is known for his extraordinary brain skills in what he accomplished in the world of physics.[8]

The list could keep going, but I'll end with my personal favorite hero in history—Abraham Lincoln. I used to read biographies on his life during my failure-soaked years! He is actually known as one who has failed perhaps the most, yet he was never derailed by it. He left for war as a captain, but returned as a private, which is the lowest military rank. He also experienced many failed attempts as a businessman. That was followed by other subsequent failures as he attempted to run for political office. Finally, he became the sixteenth President of the United States and accomplished amazing victories for America, including his remarkable leadership during the American Civil War and abolishing slavery.[9]

In closing, always remember, God can redeem any failure, whether a lifetime of sin and ruin, or a one-time tragedy of loss or failure through no fault of your own. Remember, there is life after failure, as nothing is impossible for God![10] Never give up on yourself, or on God. You never know where your failures may lead, as your best days are still ahead.

1 Romans 12:2, Ephesians 4:23; 5:26

2 Luke 22:62

3 Acts 16:27-31

4, 5, 6, 7, 8, 9 Kipman, Sebastian. "15 Highly Successful People Who Failed On Their Way To Success." Posted date unknown. *Lifehack* https://www.lifehack.org/articles/productivity/15-highly-successful-people-who-failed-their-way-success.html. Accessed October 22, 2020.

10 Genesis 18:14, Jeremiah 32:17, Matthew 19:26, Mark 10:27, Luke 1:37

GIVING THE "WHAT IF" A CHANCE

What if...there really a light at the end of this long, dark tunnel?

What if....there really is a hope to be had?

What if...there really is a peace to be found?

What if...there really is some joy down the road?

What if...God really does love unconditionally?

What if...forgiveness really is possible?

What if...acceptance by the One Whose opinion matters most really is available?

What if...there really is a second chance after failure?

What if…this hopeless situation could change given some more time?

What if…I could find new life and not die as my only way out?

To end our lives in self-appointed time is to extinguish all these possibilities that are, objectively speaking, ripe with powerful potential.

A healing agent in any relationship is when one, who has perhaps been wounded or misunderstood, taken advantage of in some way, gives the other person the benefit of the doubt. So, "what if" we could give ourselves this same gift of mercy? Many of us are hardest of all on ourselves. Therefore, it is likely possible that one of the first steps out of our painful closed-in feeling would be to give our own lives the benefit of the doubt. That is, to say a word of kindness to ourselves, "Maybe I do have a reason to live after all. Maybe I do want to believe there is hope and promise beyond all this pain. Even if in microscopic measure for now, maybe there is something slightly detectable and deep within me that does admit that I really do not want to die; I just want the pain to stop." In a creative approach, we have to treat ourselves with compassion, almost as if we're on the outside looking upon someone else's suffering. I Corinthians 13:7 says that love believes the best of every person. I dare you to consider just how worth loving and living you really are! What if it's true? It is, I promise. Moreover, God promises you are worth fighting for, since He already considered you worth dying for. Yes, your worth is reflected in the highest price He paid of sacrificing His only Son on the Cross.

Giving hope a chance is a big leap of faith in itself. Be assured, it is noticed and rewarded by God. After all, He is a rewarder of those who diligently seek Him.[1] So making the initial choice to give life another chance is the first step in that direction. Behind each of those what-if statements points to one of the greatest motivations to stay in the human race: hope. It can propel us forward when everything else within us screams from pain and exhaustion, or tempts us just to throw it all away and give up, calling ourselves "hopeless."

God's Word says that our hope *in Him* will not be disappointed or put to shame.[2] Humanly speaking, we may have experienced such a degree of pain, hardship, and suffering in life to have become a bit hardened with cynicism at this verse. After all, it seems to us that our hope has *already* been disappointed, or else we would not be so fiercely tempted with suicide in the first place. God has a different view, grander perspective, and meaning behind what He is saying.

Perhaps it requires us to look a little deeper, to what the source of our hope has actually been. What have we been trusting in as our hope and security in this life? Is it our own abilities, our jobs/careers, possessions, families, friends, or anything else besides Jesus Himself? If so, it all differs from Him in one way—it can all fail; whereas He cannot fail. Giving the "What if" a chance has everything to do with taking an honest inventory of what our source, foundation, or focus of our hope has been.

Because so much of this book, if not all, has been birthed from personal experience of having walked through every written word myself, some are older chapters than others. Well, as I returned to this particular one during my editing work, I had ironically lived out this very test of faith and hope just last month and again last week. That is, I really thought my hope was solely in God, for example, as my Provider. However, when I received a string of bad news all within two months of each other of significant financial loss, it caused me to realize that maybe I had allowed my trust and hope to be in earthly means instead of solely in God as my Provider like I had assumed. I was rather shaken and convicted; but it felt so good, as hard and upsetting as it initially was to accept, to get my eyes refocused on God being my sole Source and Provider. "All my fountains are in You!" as the Psalmist exclaims (Psalm 87:7 NIV). I had to give a hard look at the question, "What if I face even more loss; or also, what if I gain it back? Will my hope still remain fixed and stable in Jehovah Jireh being my Provider either way? The only hope He guarantees is when it is in Himself, not some earthly source as our hope. Still, I know how volatile it can be to have this awareness come into view—that our hope is unstable at best when we have our trust in anything or anyone but God Himself.

Like the rest of this book, timeless truths have to be revisited and often retested when life hits us with hard blows. It never shakes our God though, because His is an unshakeable kingdom. "Therefore, since we are receiving a kingdom that cannot be shaken, let us be thankful, and so worship God acceptably with reverence and awe, for our God is a consuming fire" (Hebrews 12:28-29 NIV). Remember, Paul tells us how important it is to renew our minds, "Do not conform any longer to the pattern of this world, but be transformed by the renewing of your mind. Then you will be able to test and approve what God's will is—His good, pleasing and perfect will" (Romans 12:2 NIV). None of us are beyond this! Here are some other great reminders to help us stay focused on keeping our hope based in the stability and eternal, lasting value of God alone—no other earthly source that can easily change or fail.

> "And this hope will not lead to disappointment. For we know how dearly God loves us, because He has given us the Holy Spirit to fill our hearts with His love" (Romans 5:5 NLT).

> "As the Scripture says, 'Anyone who trusts in Him will never be disappointed" (Romans 10:11 NCV).

> "To You, O Lord, I lift up my soul. O my God, I trust in You; Let me not be ashamed; Let not my enemies triumph over me" (Psalm 25:1-2 NKJV).

> "Sustain me according to your promise, and I will live; do not let my hopes be dashed. Uphold me, and I will be delivered; I will always have regard for Your decrees" (Psalm 119:116-117 NIV).

Our own physical bodies can deteriorate or be forever changed in an accident, thus crashing our hopes in all abilities that we had worked a lifetime to improve and succeed. Employers and economy status can change even abruptly with no warning. We saw this shocking reality during the covid-19 crisis. Consider a former example on 9-11, when the Twin Towers in New York City were attacked, crumbling empires of success and prosperity to Ground Zero all in mere moments of time, causing a profound sense of grief and loss for so many all at once—lives in massive count disrupted, ended, and families forever changed. Is our hope in material gain? Natural disasters, such as recent wildfires out West and devastating hurricanes in the Southeastern United States can erode all we have ever hoped in along these lines too. The list could continue.

Nothing is stable or secure in this world; it is why those of us who have accepted Jesus as Savior have the promise of a better one to come. This is but a mere temporary place to live. Our own bodies and abilities are not even worth counting on, because they can fail at any given moment, as subject as we all are to disease, accident, or even sudden death. While this seems so grim, and truly is for those who have no hope of heaven through accepting Jesus as Savior, we find a much deeper source of Hope that actually is promised to last forever, and never change, falter, or fail at all. It is the Hope of Jesus Himself. His name actually means "Savior." This deliverance that we find in Him is the hope that is promised never to disappoint or be put to shame.

Tying this all together, as we see that behind all the "What if" questions, the real answer is, will we be willing to have our eyes opened to what our hopes have been in or based upon? Once we establish them to be anchored in the true foundation of Jesus, all these "What if" questions actually point to giving God a chance to work in our lives to redeem, restore, and rebuild our lives. Thus, the answer to every "What if" statement is found by asking the most important question: "Will we give God a chance?" He has promised in Romans 8:28 to work out all things together for our good as we love Him. I've been told, the only way to fail is to give up. I admonish you, never give up! Let God demonstrate His greatness in how He can answer these "What if" questions in your life. You are so special to Him. He wants to do this for you!

You may be asking, as I did when so deep in my pit of depression, even if I did dare myself to believe there is a light at the end of this tunnel, how do I get there? Let me encourage you by taking this first practical step that you can start today. You will actually find that the process of doing this generates hope in itself, which becomes progressive to acquiring more strength behind your hope! Get a Scripture to hold onto that boldly confronts whatever struggle you're having or every fear you're facing. Gather verses of courage and strength to replace weakness and insecurity, or ones of comfort when you feel totally alone and forsaken. If facing financial stress, loss, or uncertainty, anchor yourself in verses that point to God as Provider. When that enemy rises, direct the Sword of the Spirit (which is the Word—

your weapon of truth) to refute all his lies. You will find your fears becoming weaker and weaker as you deliberately go the opposite way of truth, no matter how difficult it is to begin. "Feed your faith and your fears will starve."[3] One by one, you will get your "What if" questions answered by discovering how much hope there really is for you in every area of your life.

---

1 Hebrews 11:6

2 Romans 5:5

3 Max Lucado

YOUR SHIFT IS COMING

In this chapter, I'm going to share from my own experience with candid vulnerability how God set me completely free from many years of struggling with suicidal ideation and depression. While you may be tempted to dismiss one person's experience, assuming you are too far gone for it to become your own, I would gently remind you that God Himself has said that He is no respecter of persons.[1] Take courage in daring to believe that what He can do for one person, He can do for you too!

Although my memories about it are not sharp, I did struggle with childhood depression. I was taken to a child psychologist as early as age five, and to another one during my fourth grade year. Sexual abuse had taken place, but because I was threatened, I refused to talk about it. In spite of having plenty friends with whom I did enjoy playing as a little girl, and absolutely loved staying at my grandparents' house, I'm told that I often just sat on the sofa sucking my thumb in a depressed state. So the beginnings of depression had taken root quite early.

However, it was when I experienced a profound loss at age fifteen that the intensity of depression worsened. By age sixteen, life had lost its appeal altogether. It was then that the suicidal thoughts began, tormenting my mind with a pervasively nagging desire to die for many years thereafter as I battled clinical depression.

Throughout a relentless struggle with anorexia and bulimia, which began in my early teenage years and lasted twenty-five years, I very often uttered the phrases: "I just want to die. I don't want to live. God, please, I beg You to let me die." My behaviors followed accordingly. I did not realize quite the fierce stronghold that was gaining ground in my life as I was becoming ensnared by the words of my own mouth.[2]

We are told in the Word that death and life are in the power of the tongue.[3] God gives us the same decision that He gave His people in Old Testament times. "I have set before you life and death, blessings and curses. Now, choose life, so that you and your children may live" (Deuteronomy 30:19 NIV). We must make the deliberate choice each day "whom [we] will serve" (Joshua 24:15 NIV). It cannot be both life and death, since the two are at opposite extremes. Nor can we passively just exist and call that living, because to be passive is in itself a choice of apathetically shirking the responsibility of pursuing life.

This defined my problem indeed. I was living such a contradiction. I loved God with all my heart (or so I thought); and because I found His Word to be my only one piece of hope, I read and studied it quite a lot. I even memorized many verses, since I kept a pocket-sized spiral notebook of Bible verses to help while eating, for example, to combat the outrageous tormenting struggle I had with anorexia for so long. This was truly how I survived and never gave into suicide, no matter how fiercely strong the temptation of it was. It's just that I was living through such intense emotional pain that my broken heart yearned for release and relief from it. This included both past scarring and trauma that proved quite difficult to overcome and heal from the lingering effects, as well as the ongoing circumstances that were equally damaging. On the one hand, I was seeking to deepen my relationship with God, as well as all the attempts at counseling and inpatient treatment in trying to recover and "live." All the while, however, I kept uttering my desire to die. Obviously, this created such inner conflict that prohibited me from going forward, since my heart was so divided and not in complete agreement and unity with God's Word.

Even though I was very isolated from all friends and family, by God's grace alone, the lines of communication were kept open with my mother, albeit long distance. Many times, I would call her in hysterics, completely panicked and engulfed with raging despair, blurting out how much I wanted to die, and felt tempted to "end it all." I cannot imagine how overwhelming and sad that must have been for her to hear; yet her resilient responses not only melted my heart each time, but taught me a powerful lesson. Rather than attempting to reason with me at a time when I was not in my right mind enough to be reasonable anyway, she simply but authoritatively started praying the Name of Jesus into my ear as I held the phone. Sometimes it took quite a long time for me to stop sobbing and calm down, but eventually I would. She would rebuke a spirit of death and suicide, commanding it to leave in Jesus' Name. As I would listen to her praying that the love of God would invade the place where I was, my heart would soften. God's Word would do the necessary work; because "He sends forth His Word and heals them and rescues them from the pit and destruction" (Psalm 107:20 AMPC). I wish I had a dime for every time she said that verse to me! It proved oh so true. Also, He says that His Word always produces the effect for which it is sent, and never returns void (Isaiah 55:11). Furthermore, her specific mention of the love of God was the key Sword of warfare in the Word as well, because we are told, "Perfect love casts out fear….and expels every trace of terror. Fear brings with it the thought of punishment, torment; so he who is afraid has not yet reached the full maturity of love" (I John 4:18 AMP).

She interceded for me continually, and hell's wrath to kill me, even using my own behaviors to accomplish it, was stayed by the powerful sway of her prayers. You may not have anyone praying for you, but you do now. I have personally been praying for you, *every* reader of this book; as I have been in the jaws of this certain temptation, thus feel tremendous compassion for where you are. I know what it feels like to be so despairing and tempted, how powerfully strong it can be. So with great emphasis, let me say it again, "He sends forth His Word and heals *you* and rescues *you* from the pit and destruction" (Psalm 107:20 AMPC, emphasis mine).

I am by no means giving a formula here; nor can I be held liable or legally responsible for anyone's life in terms of suicide. This is not professional advice. It is simply a sharing of my own experience as an encouragement of what vital pieces were part of my ultimate victory over this particular struggle. To hear the Name of Jesus spoken so authoritatively, along with the Sword of the Spirit which is the Word of God, including the specific mention of His love, eventually did diffuse the torment that would arise for me in this certain suicide temptation. However, in my case, it was not the total story behind my final victory. Another essential step was required of me that not only conquered each subsequent battle, but ultimately won the war. That is, my own mouthpiece had to be involved in an overt, deliberate choice of a way for life to conquer death.

You may be thinking, "I want to die too much to choose life. I don't even want to live; why would I make a choice for life when it is death that I want instead?" That is precisely what I thought and felt! This did not come overnight for me at all. Plus, I admit that I went back and forth on my own attempts to speak the truth and "choose life" many times, which was exactly why my struggle with this lasted so long. I wish I could tell you the date, but I cannot. In my case, it was so gradual that I only realized just how permanent my freedom from this truly was in hindsight, after I had been living for years as utterly and completely free. So all of this is written in a reflective sense of tracking my own journey with the heart and hand of how God worked, and the instruments He used. Being such a finite human being though, I may still be unaware, and therefore unable to tell, what all He must have used and added to all I'm knowingly sharing here.

The shift began when I started voicing, "I will not die; instead, I will live to tell what the Lord has done" (Psalm 118:17 NLT). Believe it or not, this was not once the desire to live came; I do know that much about the timing! I was still rather struggling with the ambivalence of suicide temptation versus the desire to please and obey God, while admittedly being torn in the middle. Even so, I was growing indescribably desperate to get rid of the torment of that certain temptation that I was willing to try anything to overcome it. The pain of it truly was so dark and gut-wrenching that I often felt afraid of myself at times. I had already tried it all—suicide hotlines, emails to long distance friends whom I thought I could trust, antidepressant medication or other supplements, and books on depression. The same pit kept swallowing me in its abyss. That is, until I gave the all-powerful Name of Jesus and the Sword of the Word a distinctively verbal chance to save my life. The key for me was in being deliberately and audibly vocal with the truth that would finally set me free. Even though the painful temptation arose so often that the will to live was still weaker than my desire to die at the time, I kept trying to say this certain verse out loud, although sometimes no louder than a faint whisper. "I will not die; instead, I will live to tell what the Lord has done" (Psalm 118:17 NLT).

Just like I cannot offer a set time of beginning, neither can I place a definite end on when total freedom came. However, I can boldly testify that little by little this specific verse began to play louder in my head than the former phrases of my desire to die. "Replacement," as this could aptly be called, is exactly what took place. Life began overcoming death through the power of my own tongue as the Name of Jesus was releasing me from the tenacious hold the spirit of death and suicide had had over me for so long. I eventually became free from its grip altogether! So free indeed did I become that I actually found myself shocked one day as I realized for the first time in the latter half of my life that I was actually *wanting* to live for a change, not just attempting to surrender or submit to it as an act of my will! I discovered such an amazing sense of peace, hope, and joy with this that I had never before known, which must be why David ends his own sentence with what he will do with his living, and not dying—"proclaim the works of the Lord!" That is all I want to do too! The motivation to write this very book was born in the same sentence of David's becoming my own: "I will live, and not die, and proclaim the works of the Lord" indeed; because now, I yearn for other tormented souls to find this secret of joy in living free from such a dark prison of suicide temptation.

As it has now been years of walking in freedom from this certain struggle, a true testament to the totality of liberty that Jesus gives us by His truth is that now, I can hardly imagine why it took me so long to begin deliberately choosing life. Now, I cannot fathom why I would have chosen to remain in such darkness when there was so much bright light and life available that could only come when I would stop fearing life, or resenting and wanting an end to its pain, so as to make a conscious effort to speak this line of truth instead of my death wish. Your shift of genuine joy and desire to conquer this tormenting beast, and even *want* to live is coming too, if you are willing to give truth a chance to set you free! Verbalize that you will choose life and your shift into freedom from this torment *will* come.

---

1 Acts 10:34, Romans 2:11

2 Proverbs 6:2

3 Proverbs 18:21

4 John 8:32

THE "I" IN S-U-I-C-I-D-E

Although people are trying to help shake some sense into us, as they perceive we need, some of the most hurtful comments I've come across, especially in acute times of suffering, include: "Get over yourself. It's not about you. Someone else in the world has it worse than you, so be grateful for what you do have, it could be worse. Count your blessings." Perhaps statements like these have been as arrows in your own heart already, which ironically seem to exacerbate our pain and intensify the temptation.

In my own case, what would hurt even more than the statements themselves would be the fact that the speaker of them invariably did not know the extent of my situation; so it felt much like a false accusation and lack of understanding. Jesus doesn't take it lightly when others condemn us. One of the most moving stories in the Word shows His tender response of intervention when an angry mob brought a woman to be publicly exposed and stoned. She no doubt felt painfully sorry enough and condemned for her sin as it was, even to possible despair. Jesus knew not only all she was feeling, but all the details of her story too. He was quite aware of the extent of her sin—far more than her accusers were—but He turned them all away; as He showed her only mercy, grace, and pardoning love. This is to demonstrate in a literal sense how God handles situations where we are being judged. Matthew 7:1 tells us to judge not, lest we be judged. In many cases, people may sincerely be trying to help by the proverbial way of "knocking some sense" into us! Like the accused woman hurting in her silence and shame, we have to let Jesus—our Righteous Judge and Vindicator—intervene and set us free.

It is extremely important that we guard our hearts in such cases, refusing the baits of offense and bitterness; because that only invites strongholds of further pain and bondage. Honestly, if we can learn to see such shortsighted advice givers with compassion in light of how they might someday face their own breaking point, and not hold it against them that they don't understand yet, we will begin the freeing pathway out of our own self-focused miseries.

Unfortunately, it took me so many years to make this particular turn. Denial had been my coping mechanism for a long while in this way, pointing to the other person as the problem instead of myself! However, as the years of struggling kept revealing deeper layers of my own heart, I realized—with great pain—that perhaps I really was just too self-absorbed, no matter how much I could justify my plight. It was such a hard realization to see, but it did help provide a pivotal turning point in my recovery; and it was actually in very small, simple ways that God brought the truth home to my heart in order to set me free.

For example, the simplest errands presented a gigantic challenge during my deepest, darkest bondage of isolation, severe depression, and agoraphobia/paranoia struggles. Thus, after lengthy periods of procrastination and dread, once I would finally make it to the store, I would quietly observe the cashier and find my mind wondering what her life might be like. Was she a single mother trying hard to make ends meet with maybe more than one job, yet still barely enough to supply food and diapers for her kids? I would watch her arms and hands move my items wearily through the scanner, and observe how exhausted she seemed. In fact, little did she know that I had a profound amount of admiration and respect for her; as I so often found myself thinking, "I could never do what she's doing. This simple errand has thoroughly drained me for the entire day." Next, my eyes would drift to the man looking so worn in another check-out lane, ready to purchase a case of beer. "What kinds of stress and pain is he seeking desperately to escape?" I wondered. He looks so hopeless and tired—possessing that same blank stare that so many people seem to have when life has rolled over them like a bulldozer, and they are just trying to cope in whatever ways they can find.

This does not even yet bring into account all the obvious "worse comparisons" such as all the tragedies and catastrophes experienced worldwide, or the starving children in Africa, and whatever else the headlines in today's news entail. Comparisons are foolish in the first place according to II Corinthians 10:12. In God's eyes, we all matter with equal importance, just as the sparrows do. He considers our specific burdens to be proportionate in terms of what He alone knows we are capable of handling. We simply cannot afford to measure our worth, our suffering, our lives—in any way—against anyone else; because that diminishes our unique individual portrait that God says is tattooed on the palm of His hands, and is ever before Him as very special, and dearly loved. He truly cares how we hurt, and is not comparing you to me, or her to him, or us to them! Thus, we should not draw such comparisons either.

At the same time, it can bring quite a bit of fresh, open air to the suffocated mind dealing with dark, suicidal temptation and pressure to realize there really is some truth to the fact that I am on my own mind too much when it seems that my death is the only way to eliminate the pain in my life. This is the signaling banner that should wave some freedom into our minds, not condemnation or guilt. We have enough of the latter as it is. But the reality is, when our desperation, pain, suffering, and other pressuring difficulties tempt us to believe that our dying is the only way out, we are definitely crossing that line of having only ourselves on our minds; and this leads only to further pain.

As we are lured by a way out of our misery, we become all too easily enticed by relief that we forget how the consequences of our actions will negatively affect others. It's common to feel that our family or friends would be better off without us, that we are only a financial or physical burden, and other justifications. However, from an objective point of view, this cannot be true at all. Death forcibly inflicts grief onto people, which is quite a severe wound, especially if unexpected, and even when the relationship was not considered close or even all that good. It is tampering with God's place; and that invites troubling consequences even for the innocent, as everyone is definitely affected. Surely we are not so deceived to think we are actually doing anyone a favor—except ourselves, which is the point. We have become much too self-focused when we begin entering this ever so narrow tunnel of seeking only our own relief, to the detriment of others. We did not enter this world without it affecting others in some way; nor can we leave it without others being affected.

Even if you are convinced that no one would care, because maybe you have no family at all, or the one you do have seemingly cares nothing about your life, once again, consider Jesus. A broader view does exist, and it is a compelling one. We do not own our own destinies, any more than we own other people's destinies either. When we willingly choose to inflict the shock and pain of grief upon other people, even if they are simply nearby neighbors or distant acquaintances that we think would not even notice, the truth of the matter is, we are attempting to play God; and we simply don't have that right. People do care and do notice far more than we realize. If you read in tomorrow's paper that your neighbor committed suicide, or even just attempted it, would you not instantly flash back into your mind what the months were like at that house? Was anything different or noticeably wrong, wondering if you could you have done something, even if you had not even known the person?

By contrast, it might be that part of your temptation to attempt suicide is, in fact, a cry to be heard or noticed. It may be that your pain has taken such a toll on you emotionally that you cannot think of any other creative way than to yell drastically with this fatal action instead of constructively seeking other ways of communication to get your needs met. Believe me, I heard this lie in my head too. Again, without a trace of condemnation, I appeal to the heart of you that would consider the other side—the side of the receiving end to your action. It is by far the harder way to reach out for help in a healthy, proper way, but in reality, this is definitely the self-less route; whereas suicide—even as a cry for help or to be noticed or heard—is only the "I" in s-u-I-c-I-d-e (i.e. self on the mind) mattering most. Said in utmost love and compassion as one who has truly been there, I know how much it hurts to be accused of selfishness; so my heart behind this book is to eradicate the condemnation in the first place, as that truly only drives one closer to it! However, I had personally broken down so much that I had no other choice than to come face to face with the harsh reality that maybe I really did have my "self" on my mind too much to be objective, no matter how fiercely pressured I felt with the temptation, including the alluring idea that bringing myself to a quick end would naturally solve all my problems instantly.

Of course, that must be the enemy's favorite style when he tempts us with anything, not just suicide—that it will be an immediate problem-solver. Again, in the earlier point of how others are inevitably affected, problems are not solved, but are actually compounded for those we leave behind. That's the catch. Our adversary is characteristically impatient, always pushy and forceful, no matter who may get hurt in the process. Our Savior is by nature always utterly patient, gentle, and defines Himself as Love, "God is love" and "Love is patient, love is kind" (I John 4:8, I Corinthians 13:4 NIV). Love does not harm anyone. The enemy's promises are predictably empty and come up short each and every time. God's promises, on the other hand, are so solid and worthy of staking our entire lives upon that He even says they *already* have their fulfillment in Jesus Christ. They *always* find their "yes" and "amen" through Jesus, meaning that they are never void, empty, or fail to deliver; but are completely reliable each and every time.

In fact, the way God puts it to us like this gives us such a warm welcome to believe Him at His Word that *He* will be the One to come through for us. We do not have to take matters into our own hands after all. We can actually find so much freedom in forgetting about ourselves, focusing on *Him*, and watching Him fulfill His own work, His own Word, and His own promises in our lives as we simply exalt Him higher than ourselves and our own thoughts. Jude 1:24 says, "Now unto Him that is able to keep you from falling, and to present you faultless before the presence of His glory with exceeding joy…" One of the biggest reliefs came for me when I realized the weight of all my burdens in life were truly never meant to be carried in my own strength. Getting myself off my mind was so freeing, because self-absorption and all its tormenting worry is such a miserable prison. My life and the outcome of it could all be "off my mind" in the sense of casting all my care on Jesus because He cares for us.[1] He knows what we need; if He cares for the sparrows, seeing to it that their needs are met, how much more does He know what our needs are, along with the power to meet them like no one else can. Ephesians 3:20 inspires us with great hope to believe in God's ability instead of focusing on our limits and inadequacies, "Now to Him Who is able to do immeasurably more than all we ask or imagine, according to His power that is at work within us." Not even our perfection or progress is all on our shoulders. It liberated me so much to discover that my life is God's project! My repeated failures and human flaws do not catch God off guard at all. Instead of wallowing in shame for how we've blown it, we can trust our Master to redeem our mess; I promise He can!

Have you ever tried repeatedly to break free from a habit or addiction, but the harder you tried, the more you failed? It's because the more focused we become on not failing, the more likely it is that we do that very thing. It's like someone saying, "Don't look down; whatever you do, do not look down!" Invariably, we are going to look down! We truly are God's work; so let Him accomplish in you what you cannot do on your own. Listen to how much pressure this takes off us: "[Not in your own strength] for it is God Who is all the while effectually at work in you [energizing and creating in you the power and desire], both to will and to work for His good pleasure and satisfaction and delight" (Philippians 2:13 AMPC). Hear the liberty in this!

When we focus on loving Jesus in light of how much He loves us—enough to purchase our lives when He literally bled to death for us—we cannot help but worship Him. As a result, He becomes bigger in our minds, while our tormenting affliction reduces in size. An old song I remember from church as a child goes something like this: "Let's forget about ourselves, magnify the Lord, and worship Him." This is the only answer that truly works when it comes to suicide temptation. The enemy wants to diminish Jesus in every way, and suicide accomplishes that indeed. Consequently, this creates a rippling effect of painful questions, confusion, and grief for others—be they family (distant or near, strained or close), mere strangers and acquaintances; and other effects that spread and stretch beyond what we do not even realize. Darkness is the result, and the enemy wickedly, coldly and simply laughs. Nobody wins, and everybody hurts. But God's Way is for us to magnify Jesus as the Light of the world, the Light in our darkness, and the Light of our salvation. As we lift Him up and forget about ourselves, somehow—only as our creative Creator can make beauty out of darkness, void, and chaos—He can turn our lives into a triumphant trophy for His glory.

We can have a renewed mind where self is no longer on the throne; and instead of our constant internal pressure to "end it all, so that this pain will be over," we can find so much contentment in letting God truly have ownership and control, since it becomes all about Him anyway. Speaking of relieving pressure, there is no greater stress relief available than to realize we are actually just an instrument in God's loving hands; our lives are not our own after all! We can deposit ourselves, and every stressor and burden we carry, into the hands of our great God; and just rest in Him, to see what He wants to do. This is literally what Jesus invites us to do: "Come to Me, all who labor and are heavy-laden *and* overburdened, and I will cause you to rest. [I will ease and relieve and refresh your souls.] Take My yoke upon you and learn of Me, for I am gentle (meek) and humble (lowly) in heart, and you will find rest (relief and ease and refreshment and recreation and blessed quiet) for your souls. For My yoke is wholesome (useful, good—not harsh, hard, sharp, or pressing, but comfortable, gracious, and pleasant), and My burden is light and easy to be borne" (Matthew 11:28-30 AMPC).

Please realize that He has such a magnificent, creative plan for your life. Most likely, you've not even considered all the possibilities of what God wants to do with you! Simply give Him a chance to do it! Lifting our eyes off our own plight to see Him high and exalted above all else is the "how to" behind living, especially beyond this painful, pressing temptation of suicide. We do not have to have all the answers. This is indeed how and why we can worship God in the first place. If we knew everything there is to know, if we owned the whole world, imagine the heavy weight of responsibility this would entail. Impossible! Not for God though. He thrives on taking responsibility for His own. We get to take a big, deep breath and rest! Just as God thrives to be in His sovereign position, we are at our best when we fully surrender all the controls, the need to know and understand, and simply enter His rest by believing, trusting, and worshipping Him. *He* is the One taking care of us—to the very end, which He alone gets to determine!

> "After you have suffered for a little while, the God of all grace, who called you to His eternal glory in Christ, will Himself perfect, confirm, strengthen and establish you" (I Peter 5:10 NASB).

> "And He will establish you to the end [keep you steadfast, give you strength, and guarantee your vindication; He will be your warrant against all accusation or indictment so that you will be] guiltless and irreproachable in the day of our Lord Jesus Christ (the Messiah). God is faithful (reliable, trustworthy, and therefore ever true to His promise, and He can be depended on); by

Him you were called into companionship and participation with His Son, Jesus Christ our Lord" (I Corinthians 1:8-9 AMPC).

"I will be the same until your old age, and I will bear you up when you turn gray. I have made you, and I will carry you; I will bear and rescue you" (Isaiah 46:4 CSB). "Praise the Lord; praise God our Savior! For each day He carries us in His arms" (Psalm 68:19 NLT).

He is, after all, the Author and *Finisher* of our faith.[2] So don't give up on Him, His work, His plan, or His timing! He makes *all things* beautiful in His time; and you definitely matter greatly in God's eyes. Turn your focus on Jesus, for He cares for you watchfully and affectionately. Make no mistake, when the enemy lies to you that the only way to be heard is to take your own life, know that Jesus is quite intimately aware of your pain. There is a better way out than suicide. His Name is Jesus. He will not let you suffer temptation greater than you can bear.

"No test or temptation that comes your way is beyond the course of what others have had to face. All you need to remember is that God will never let you down; He'll never let you be pushed past your limit; He'll always be there to help you come through it" (I Corinthians 10:13 MSG).

---

[1] I Peter 5:7

[2] Hebrews 12:2

OUTSIDERS AND OUTCASTS

Have you been rejected? The enemy has a way of twisting this certain heartache, turning it inward, convincing you that you should reject yourself through suicide. Remember, he lies! You are worthy of love and acceptance, no matter what has happened to you or what was said that broke your heart.

It can be incredibly painful to feel like an outsider or outcast especially in the context of church, where we would expect our hunger for acceptance and unconditional love to be filled. Rejection or exclusion can certainly create wounds of a deep kind. Since churches are full of mere human beings, however, we need to extend forgiveness, grace, and mercy; so that we don't become imprisoned by bitterness, which will hurt and destroy far more than this rejection pain. Even so, we can move forward in the freedom of God's unconditional acceptance of us. The most helpful salve for this particular wound is to encourage ourselves in the Lord with what His own Word says on this matter.

To Jesus, outsiders and outcasts were extremely important, to the point that He literally sought them out with messages of love, redemption, hope, and acceptance! After all, He left the ninety-nine and went after the one in the parable of the lost sheep. In John 4, He also went out of His way, making the socially unacceptable journey *through* Samaria, where Jews never went, just because a certain woman was on His mind that needed His loving acceptance and redemptive message of hope. She was definitely an outcast. In fact, just to go into town for water, she had to navigate her trail to the well wisely, basically in hiding by going at an off-time, so as to avoid the others that went there at more typical times of day. She had reason to be ashamed, but Jesus wasn't turned off by this. He saw the deepest need of her heart was far more important than compromising His reputation just by talking with her. He was always doing things like this that ruffled the feathers of those judgmental onlookers, ready to criticize and mock Him for such actions that were propelled by His unstoppable love. She mattered deeply to Jesus. So do you.

When I went through my own fire of feeling like an outsider and outcast from the exclusivity of church friends I had cherished for years, it was absolutely one of the most painful experiences of my life. However, as I drank deeply from the Well of Living Water of Truth in God's Word, I found that what I experienced from people in this context versus what experience God was offering me by His Word of Truth were drastically different. This gradually brought such deep healing and liberated me that I cannot help but share the nuggets of gold I found.

Before I share such hope though, let me first disclose the new outpourings of my experience. First, this may enable you a chance to relate and feel understood. Secondly, these various expressions will help us appreciate all the more what a rich, lasting comfort we have in our friendship with Jesus. This was a journaled prayer of mine during a period of experiencing pain in the church, thrust into a place of not knowing who to trust. I had titled it, "Let the Oppressed Go Free."

> *Jesus, You see how strongly my tears are flowing again today. Only You are aware of how deeply I hurt, and how crushed to the marrow my soul has been with the bruising of grief, sorrow, brokenness, and pain. Ever so naturally I have given way to guilt and shame as if I am being harshly driven to my utter ruin by taskmasters to which I've been too oppressed, crushed, broken, and intimidated to stand up for my own defense. I have been much too low to rise, as my enemies have tormented me night*

and day. I have repented until I'm sore inside—countless times—which, standing alone, states the explicit problem. I must find You and enter into Your rest. After all, in Your last dying breaths on the cross, hanging there in the Blood-shedding Sacrifice of brutal torture as You purchased our hope of redemption, You uttered in earth-shattering voice: "It is finished." Oh my Lord, make me new as I breathe Your life-giving salvation into me just now. It is not only an eternal salvation that Your Blood shed made possible, but a daily salvation and deliverance that my heart can find in You at every point of need and desire. It hurts in the deepest way to be shunned—cast out, unforgiven, and unloved; but because I'm entirely too desperate and destitute to listen to the painful blows of reality, I relentlessly press in deeper and closer to the rhythm of Your Voice, Your heart, and Your Word. This has been the kind of oppression that has nearly suffocated the life right out of me. My only hope is to live based on what Your Word says, that I can be forgiven and set free by Your Truth. If I go the way of how I feel, I'll surely die. Lord, I have been wounded to the very core of my soul. My heart breaks a little more everyday. I don't know when I've needed Your healing quite so much. Maybe all this torturous pain is likened to sharing in Your death—which will be followed by sharing in Your resurrection life. Oh Jesus, You are my resounding hope, my Song in this dark night, my Light and Salvation, my Deliverer. You are my Redeemer, Bright and Morning Star, and my enduring, unconditional Love.

I did find all I needed in Jesus as I encountered His powerfully comforting presence. When the Psalmist was feeling like so much evil had attempted to surround and defeat him, feeling so alone even to the point of perceiving God to be far away, he commands his own soul to remember the absolute truth, "You have seen it; yes, You note trouble and grief (vexation) to requite it with Your hand. The unfortunate commits himself to You; You are the helper of the fatherless" (Psalm 10:14 AMPC).

Interestingly, I found this two months after my dad died, when my soul connected immediately to his "fatherless" word; but then over time, it continued to fit in so many other situations (losses, rejection, deep soul wounds) where I felt altogether alone and abandoned, full of grief and vexation. It has always brought comfort to me to know that nothing escapes God's careful notice; moreover, He has promised to requite it with His hand, meaning He will return it with favor! He is on your side. He sees what you have gone through, and He will bring not only justice and help, but comfort of a matchless kind.

Don't let someone steal your crown![1] The only way we can forfeit our destiny and sense of belonging to Christ is actually not at all by what someone else says or does to us; it is if we ourselves throw it away and abandon our unique calling. Understand all that has been made rightfully yours through Jesus, and don't throw it away! "Remember that in those days you were living utterly apart from Christ; you were enemies of God's children, and He had promised you no help. You were lost, without God, and without hope. But now you belong to Christ Jesus, and though you once were far away from God, now you have been brought very near to Him because of what Jesus Christ has done for you with His blood" (Ephesians 2:12-13 TLB).

Esau gave up his birthright for a mere bowl of soup! Can you imagine? We have been given all-encompassing, unconditional love and acceptance into God's family when we receive Jesus' cleansing blood, and all that His death and resurrection made possible for us to have as members of God's own family. As piercingly painful as your rejection or excluding experience may have been in a church setting, or elsewhere that you had a longing for acceptance, please don't forfeit all that is rightfully yours as a child of God for a mere bowl of soup, as it were, such as some temporal earthly pleasure that seems to numb the pain for now. Hebrews 10:35 tells us not to fling away our confidence as God's own dearly loved children, indeed heirs of the Kingdom of God; for it carries with it great reward.

God says that we do belong, no matter our past history, race, color, societal status, or shortcomings and struggles. He loves us tenderly forever in a completely unconditional way. If you have received His cleansing forgiveness through the blood of Jesus, and believe in Him with all your heart, you do belong to God! You do matter so deeply to Him! In fact, Jesus says that He personally makes sure that He does not lose even one that the Holy Spirit has drawn into God's family![2] This is our hope, security, confidence, and source of our acceptance! Please don't let yourself be convinced otherwise, causing you to throw yourself or your inheritance away! God knows *no* outsider or outcasts!

Ephesians 2:19 and 21 are incredibly profound verses along these lines as we see so clearly that it is the Holy Spirit Who joins us into God's family. What power would mere man possibly have to undo or negate this work of the All-powerful Holy Spirit? If you consider the history of Jews and Gentiles, and how God operated in the unfolding of it all, you will see a dramatic picture of God's character in how He deals with outsiders and outcasts to this day. At the end of this chapter is provided an entire section from the Word to express this.

You see, Gentiles actually were the excluded ones. From the very beginning, Jews came first. Even enemies knew this. Just look how they were targeted with violence, such as the Holocaust, and the anti-Semitism that continues to our present days. Although it may seem like favoritism at first glance, it was all part of God's plan in order for His heart of mercy and grace to be demonstrated.

When He Himself experienced rejection from the Jews, He was so heartbroken by their lack of acceptance that He decided to provoke them to jealousy by grafting in the Gentiles to His amazing covenant promises. The wall of hostility between the two was utterly destroyed by the shed Blood of Jesus. As such a powerful history maker, Jesus sacrificed His own life to make peace possible and tear down the dividing wall of hostility; and by this, we see a miraculous acceptance forever in place for all who will just believe and receive in this finished work of His. We are granted access and acceptance into His love when we simply believe and receive His love and the atonement of His own Blood that made a way for us to enter into covenant with Him.

Precious child of God, no matter how or by whom you may have experienced rejection, you will never be rejected by God once you receive His gift of love. Furthermore, He can completely heal you of the pain of rejection by which you feel like an outsider or outcast. I speak from experience for sure on this point. It was a pain so deep that I never thought would heal; but remember, nothing is impossible with God! If He could comfort and heal my heart and soul from seemingly irreparable damage, He can do the same for you. Simply believe and receive.

> "Once you were under God's curse, doomed forever for your sins. You went along with the crowd and were just like all the others, full of sin, obeying Satan, the mighty prince of the power of the air, who is at work right now in the hearts of those who are against the Lord. All of us used to be just as they are, our lives expressing the evil within us, doing every wicked thing that our passions or our evil thoughts might lead us into. We started out bad, being born with evil natures, and were under God's anger just like everyone else.
>
> But God is so rich in mercy; He loved us so much that even though we were spiritually dead and doomed by our sins, He gave us back our lives again when He raised Christ from the dead—only by His undeserved favor have we ever been saved—and lifted us up from the grave into glory along with Christ, where we sit with Him in the heavenly realms—all because of what Christ Jesus did. And now God can always point to us as examples of how very, very rich His kindness is, as shown in all He has done for us through Jesus Christ.
>
> Because of His kindness, you have been saved through trusting Christ. And even trusting is not of yourselves; it too is a gift from God. Salvation is not a reward for the good we have done, so none of us can take any credit for it. It is God Himself Who has made us what we are and given us new lives from Christ Jesus; and long ages ago He planned that we should spend these lives in helping others.

Never forget that once you were heathen and that you were called godless and "unclean" by the Jews. (But their hearts, too, were still unclean, even though they were going through the ceremonies and rituals of the godly, for they circumcised themselves as a sign of godliness.) Remember that in those days you were living utterly apart from Christ; you were enemies of God's children, and He had promised you no help. You were lost, without God, without hope.

But now you belong to Christ Jesus, and though you once were far away from God, now you have been brought very near to Him because of what Jesus Christ has done for you with His blood.

For Christ Himself is our way of peace. He has made peace between us Jews and you Gentiles by making us all one family, breaking down the wall of contempt that used to separate us. By His death He ended the angry resentment between us, caused by the Jewish laws that favored the Jews and excluded the Gentiles, for He died to annul that whole system of Jewish laws. Then He took the two groups that had been opposed to each other and made them parts of Himself; thus He fused us together to become one new person, and at last there was peace. As parts of the same body, our anger against each other has disappeared, for both of us have been reconciled to God. And so the feud ended at last at the cross. And He has brought this Good News of peace to you Gentiles who were very far away from Him, and to us Jews who were near. Now all of us, whether Jews or Gentiles, may come to God the Father with the Holy Spirit's help because of what Christ has done for us.

Now you are no longer strangers to God and foreigners to heaven, but you are members of God's very own family, citizens of God's country, and you belong in God's household with every other Christian.

What a foundation you stand on now: the apostles and the prophets; and the cornerstone of the building is Jesus Christ Himself! We who believe are carefully joined together with

Christ as parts of a beautiful, constantly growing temple for God. And you also are joined with Him and with each other by the Spirit and are part of this dwelling place of God" (Ephesians 2:1-22 TLB).

---

1 Revelation 3:11

2 John 17:12

DOOR TO HOPE: FINDING A FRIEND WHO NEVER FAILS

How many times have we invested so much of our lives, our energy, our resources, and our time into relationships, only to experience the profound depth of pain, betrayal, rejection, heartache, or loss? In fact, often the "soul ties" linger as strongholds of grief or anger within us long after the relationship has ended, leaving us feeling used as damaged goods.

Or, it may simply be that the relationship has not ended at all; no overt pain has been inflicted. Rather, we just find a gnawing emptiness and lack of fulfillment as our significant other, friend, or people in general leave us wanting for something more. Is this lack of true connection with people, an intense loneliness, fueling your temptation to commit suicide? Good news for you, there is definitely a deep sense of fulfillment along these lines that doesn't have to elude you anymore. This is the Door to hope.

When you develop an intimate friendship with Jesus, truly getting to know Him for Who He really is, and how much He can identify with you in your sorrow and suffering, this certain hunger for more is satisfied at last. Finally, we realize that yes, there is indeed something more to this life. Not only is He the only One Who can truly empathize with the disappointments and anguish in being hurt, rejected, or abandoned; but He has promised to be that Friend Who "sticks closer than a brother" (Proverbs 18:24 NIV). No matter how sincere or well-meaning, people will always fail us; just as we will inevitably fail others also. The sooner we embrace this truth, we will not only be able to lower our unrealistic expectations, but when we turn our focus onto Jesus as the only One incapable of failing, the freer we will be.

When we draw from Jesus' examples in how to handle the various hurts that can happen with people, such as betrayal, rejection, mockery or sarcasm, and invalidation, we find an unshakable hope and ultimate fulfillment in *His* gift of friendship that no other source on earth can provide. Take a quiet minute and consider all your highest hopes and dreams that a great friend would entail. Would it not be someone who knows all about you, weaknesses and failures included, yet loves you unconditionally anyway? Would it not be someone with whom you could relate and identify, having shared similar experiences or who has endured the same struggles and temptations you face? Of course, Jesus is called not only our Friend, but our High Priest for a reason. "So Jesus had to become like His brothers in every way. He had to be one of us to be our Religious Leader to go between God and us. He had loving-pity on us and He was faithful. He gave Himself as a gift to die on a cross for our sins so that God would not hold these sins against us any longer. Because Jesus was tempted as we are and suffered as we do, He understands us and He is able to help us when we are tempted" (Hebrews 2:17-18 NLV). "For we do not have a High Priest who is unable to understand and sympathize and have a shared feeling with our weaknesses and infirmities and liability to the assaults of temptation, but One Who has been tempted in every respect as we are, yet without sinning" (Hebrews 4:15 AMPC).

Think about how Jesus had His closest friends around the dinner table with Him as the last meal He would have before His death. He knew even then that Judas would betray Him for mere money, and that Peter would disown and deny Him altogether. He loved them anyway. Knowing our human nature, if we had just a sense (let alone a definite knowing) that someone was about to betray or deny knowing us, we would not have even invited them to dine with us! Not Jesus.

He operated from such a heart of unconditional love all the time, even in the direct face of persecution and pain.

As we will discuss further in the next chapter, He dealt repeatedly with the heartache of invalidation too. Have you been treated as worthless? Have you felt used and then discarded as trash? Jesus is your Door to hope in this way too; He truly understands when people treat you as if you have no worth. We get our pride tested and shown for what it is when we have this overwhelming drive to prove our point, insist that we are right, or just generally look for our sense of self-worth to be validated by other people. When we are not completely humble, we easily get offended if someone condemns or belittles us. Jesus, however, was so humble and secure in knowing His identity and Kingdom purpose that He did not allow Himself to be swayed when people were condescending, mocking, sarcastic, and invalidating of Him. In fact, Isaiah 53:7 describes Him as a Lamb being led to the slaughter, and He did not even open His mouth to defend Himself. This was even right before He would be flogged, beaten, and killed all based on lies people believed! In other words, He was hurled blows of false accusation claiming He deserved death. He could have shouted back to vindicate Himself, but that wasn't in His gentle nature at all. As the old song goes, He looked beyond their faults and saw their need for eternal salvation and deliverance; and this is why He submitted Himself to be tortured, instead of proving Himself otherwise validated as someone who should not be put to death. He knew our salvation could only be made possible when He would humble Himself to become the atoning sacrifice in our place.

Notice that in spite of being the royal King of heaven and abasing Himself to take on human flesh, He never looked to mere human beings for validation in Who He was, but rather, lived out the love He had from His Father, which was good enough for His assurance. We can do the same, as we are even considered to be part of His royal priesthood![1] If we look to people for our sense of worth, they will fail us every time, sooner or later, which may cause us to lose hope. This is because our need is too deep for human beings to meet. It is not in anyone's power to give us what we need, notably a sense of worth, security, or hope. Only the Triune God—our Father, our Lord Jesus, and our amazing Comforter (Holy Spirit)—can truly fulfill and provide us with that rich confidence and surety of being worthy of love and acceptance. This gives us hope! Run through your Doorway of hope to Jesus. In Him alone, you find your worth, reason to live, and a Friend Who never fails.

Now that we see a few examples of how people inevitably fail us, just as they failed Jesus, we also look to our Savior to see the dire importance of forgiving, releasing, and even blessing those who hurt us. As a matter of fact, when we don't forgive, we actually give the enemy wide open access to our lives, which is obviously dangerous! Beloved, this secret right here might be why you want to end your life. In Ephesians 4:26, we are told that the enemy is given a stronghold when we let the sun go down on our anger. Think about how many nights you've gone to bed with a grudge, obstinately opposed or even passively ignoring the need to forgive someone who has hurt you. That's a mighty fortress of a stronghold built around your very soul such that the enemy is now imprisoning you. No more are you in control, because despair has taken control of you. This can all change, and even be prevented, once you choose to forgive, release, and even pray blessings on your offender. As you seal this in Jesus' name, the enemy absolutely must flee!

I have found in my own personal experience that the correlation with how badly I wanted to die was often tied to how bitterly wounded I felt. It was indeed a prison of torment in which I lived, yet wishing the hurtful individual would be imprisoned instead. That never works. It leads straight to despair and ruin, all the while that the enemy seeks to win greater control doing what he does best—stealing, killing, and destroying in a disastrous ripple effect. By contrast, Jesus came to give life in all its abundance. All it takes to start receiving from Jesus, our abundant Life-Giver, is to forgive each and every person who has hurt you so deeply, however far back your memories take you. Releasing them totally unto a life of blessings after you have forgiven is really important, as you will soon discover how much this actually releases you into a life of peace, joy, freedom, and blessings for yourself as well!

A clarification I discovered may help you like it did me regarding the idea of "blessing" whoever has hurt us. In a commentary written in her own study Bible, Joyce Meyer says, "To work through the process of forgiveness and enjoy the peace we week, we must do what God tells us to do, which is not only to forgive but also to bless. One reason we find it so hard to pray for those who hurt us and mistreat us is that we tend to think we are asking God to bless them physically or materially. The truth is that we are not praying for them to make more money or have more possessions; we are praying for them to be blessed spiritually. What we are doing is asking God to bring truth and revelation to them about their attitude and behavior so they will be willing to repent and be freed from their sins." She also stresses that to bless in this context means "to speak well of."[2]

This really helped me, because although I had tried to complete my forgiveness with the concept of asking God to bless the other person, it used to feel so fake and skeletal to me, without my innermost genuinely being feeling it. I struggled with how much I was still hurting, so the thought of seeing them all happy with extra blessings rubbed salt into a wound. However, Joyce Meyer's way of explaining the extra step of blessing them helped me realize that I did want God to unveil their eyes to the truth. I did want them to be blessed, and therefore, an added measure of grace was given to me such that I could authentically desire their highest good. I could speak well of them, knowing that God would make things right as my forgiveness was made complete by blessing them. The point in all this is that inevitably, people will fail and hurt us, sometimes with wounds that fester for a lifetime; but walking through the Door to hope, we find Jesus as the Friend Who never fails. Forgiving, blessing, and releasing those who have wounded us is part of walking through the Door to hope. Only then, can we experience the fullest measure of intimate friendship with Jesus.

Remember, no one can steal your joy unless you allow them; nor can anyone imprison you with the poison of bitterness and tormenting despair unless you choose this by way of unforgiveness. Let them go and embrace hope and joy, allowing Jesus to meet all your needs for approval, love, and acceptance, since no one on earth can anyway! Again, forgiveness opens a door to finding hope in Jesus. Jesus is the Door to abundant living. He embodies what true life is: Living Bread, Living Water (our survival), "Living Light" (John 8:12 TLB).

To look at the "Door of Hope" in another way, the Old Testament book of Hosea depicts the Valley of Achor, meaning "trouble." This speaks of God's heart promising restoration to His people. The Valley of Achor describes the scene of Israel's trouble, but God says that it will become a "door of hope," which is precisely what He is saying to you in your life's trouble. In this beautiful book, God paints a picture of a prostitute who has been chasing after many lovers and who would no doubt feel so used and abused as damaged goods. Nevertheless, through the portrait of what God asks Hosea to do in marrying her despite of her adulterous behavior, He shows His own heart toward us in the lengths He is willing to go in winning back our seemingly ruined lives. When we have destroyed our lives and are in trouble, God wants to open a Door of Hope for us. "There I will give her back her vineyards, and will make the Valley of Achor a door of hope. There she will respond as in the days of her youth, as in the day she came up out of Egypt" (Hosea 2:15 NIV). You may want to read the picturesque story of Hosea to see how jealous God's love is for you. Not only do you never have to fear being rejected or abandoned by God, but you will find His love for you to be of a passionately pursuing kind. This is how our hope begins, develops, and grows; because when we truly grasp the depths, unconditional quality, and permanency by which we are loved, we can hold our heads high above all shame, reproach, and past rejection.

A final thought about hope in Jesus is to consider the outcome. If you are hopeless now, in what, who, or where was your hope based that led to your lack of hope? What if you could be certain that your hope would never fail or come to that same lack? Jesus is Living! Death has been defeated. Why would we want to follow the side that we already know has lost? Would you want to invest in anything if you knew ahead of time your investment was guaranteed to fail with documented proof? Of course not! Yet this is exactly what foolish choice we make when we go the way of suicide. It is the enemy's losing side to which we lose our entire life savings, or investment, if you will. The Word (as our documented proof from an omniscient [all-knowing] source) has already told us that the enemy loses in the end! Actually, he is defeated even now, although he keeps trying to convince us otherwise. On the other hand, we can be on the winning side when we receive Jesus as Savior; for our documented proof of His victory is in how He says the following in His own Word.

"Greater is He in us than he who is in the world" (I John 4:4).

"These things I have spoken to you, so that in Me you may have peace. In this world you have tribulations, but take courage; I have overcome the world" (John 16:33 NASB).

Whereas the enemy came only to steal, kill, and destroy, Jesus came to give us life more abundantly.[3] After all, God invested all that is living into us when He blew His own breath into our newborn lungs at birth. Then Jesus sacrificed His own flesh to pour out holy Blood to invest into our hearts the gift of choosing eternal life. On that very day, in fact, the enemy was conquered as he was made a footstool for Jesus' feet. If you were at a royal dining table, would you choose to sit in the seat prepared for you beside the King with your other privileged brothers and sisters, where you rightfully belong as part of your inheritance; or would you crawl under the table to the dark place underneath the footstool of the King's feet? The Door to Hope begins when you realize that you were bought with this costliest Blood of Christ such that it is your new identity. You no longer have to wear the cloak of shame or the face of a rejected outcast. The kind of hope I'm talking about here is of a lasting, unchanging kind. It is actually so solid that it was sealed as an oath. Listen to how the authoritative Word of God describes it.

> "Accordingly God also, in His desire to show more convincingly and beyond doubt to those who were to inherit the promise the unchangeableness of His purpose and plan, intervened (mediated) with an oath. This was so that, by two unchangeable things [His promise and His oath] in which it is impossible for God ever to prove false or deceive us, we who have fled to Him for refuge might have mighty indwelling strength and strong encouragement to grasp and hold fast the hope appointed for us and set before us.
>
> Now we have this hope as a sure and steadfast anchor of the soul [it cannot slip and it cannot break down under whoever steps out upon it—a hope] that reaches further and enters into the very certainty of the Presence within the veil, where Jesus has entered in for us [in advance]…having become a High Priest forever…" (Hebrews 6:17-20 AMPC).

Final thoughts on our Door of Hope is that Jesus even calls Himself the Door for the sheep, indicating how much care and protection with which He guards His own. He is called our Good Shepherd for a beautiful reason. Listen to Him describe the powerful meaning for you as you hear the hope in His voice.

> "'Truly, truly I say to you, he who does not enter by the door into the sheepfold, but climbs up some other way, is a thief and a robber. But he who enters by the door is the shepherd of the sheep. To him the doorkeeper opens, and the sheep hear his voice. He calls his own sheep by name, and he leads them out. When he brings out his own sheep, he goes before them. And the sheep follow him, for they know his voice. Yet they will never follow a stranger, but will run away from him. For they do not know the voice of strangers.' Jesus told them this parable, but they did not understand what He was telling them.

Then Jesus said to them again, 'Truly, truly I say to you, I am the door of the sheep. All who came before Me are thieves and robbers, but the sheep did not listen to them. I am the door. If anyone enters through Me, he will be saved and will go in and out and find pasture. The thief does not come, except to steal and kill and destroy. I came that they may have life, and that they may have it more abundantly.

I am the good shepherd. The good shepherd lays down His life for the sheep. But he who is a hired hand, and not a shepherd, who does not own the sheep, sees the wolf coming, and leaves the sheep, and runs away. So the wolf catches the sheep and scatters them. The hired hand runs away because he is a hired hand and does not care about the sheep.

I am the good shepherd. I know My sheep and am known by My own. Even as the Father knows Me, so I know the Father. And I lay down My life for the sheep. I have other sheep who are not of this fold. I must also bring them, and they will hear My voice. There will be one flock and one shepherd. Therefore My Father loves Me, because I lay down My life that I may take it up again. No one takes it from Me, but I lay it down Myself. I have power to lay it down, and I have power to take it up again. I received this command from My Father...'

Jesus answered them, '...My sheep hear My voice, and I know them, and they follow Me. I give them eternal life. They shall never perish, nor shall anyone snatch them from My hand. My Father, who has given them to Me, is greater than all. No one is able to snatch them from My Father's hand'" (John 10:1-30 MEV).

---

1 I Peter 2:9

2 Meyer, Joyce. *The Everyday Life Bible Containing the Amplified Old Testament and the Amplified New Testament*. "Notes and Commentary." First Edition. New York, NY: Faith Words, 2006. Pg 1618.

3 John 10:10

INVALIDATION

Even though the issue of being validated was mentioned in the previous chapter, I wanted to develop the topic a bit further. After all, it can be such a powerfully painful component that tempts many of us with suicide as a way of finally being heard or validated by those who matter most to us.

To glean some truth from another story in the Old Testament, let's take a look at Leah. Remember, she was Rachel's sister. The story has it that Rachel was clearly the more attractive one. First of all, this had to hurt deeply for Leah. Her own father, Laban, had tricked Jacob into marrying her. It was a broken promise on top of trickery and conniving manipulation—all because he realized Leah would be less desirable to a potential mate, and therefore harder for him to marry off, as was the customary role for fathers back then.

If you need a refresher on this story, here is a brief recap. Jacob was one of Isaac's sons who discovered this beautiful girl named Rachel. Immediately, he was head over heels for her, so he wanted to ask her father (Laban) for permission to marry her. Laban only conditionally granted his request as he required Jacob to work for him seven years before he could marry Rachel. Since Jacob was convinced that Rachel was worth it as the one he wanted of the two sisters, he fulfilled his end of the bargain—only to be deceived by Laban in being given Leah instead. This was even after Laban changed the terms and conditions, doubling the time period for Jacob to work for him, which he also had completed. However, through further deception, he still ended up with Leah, the less desired, unwanted one.

The Bible makes it obvious that Rachel was gorgeous, explaining Jacob's strong attraction to her. Leah's only pretty feature was her eyes, yet sadly, this did nothing for Jacob. She was invalidated by the one whose opinion mattered most to her—her husband's. It did not stop there. The one great gift that Leah could give her husband that Rachel could not offer was her fertility.

Leah had spent so much time and effort trying to get Jacob's attention. Even so, nothing worked—not even having the sons Jacob wanted. Thus, when Judah was born, and he still didn't validate her by loving her, she threw up her hands, so to speak, and altogether quit trying to earn his favor, affection, and validation. She simply said, "This time I will praise the Lord" (Genesis 29:35). In a book titled, *Jealousy—The Sin No One Talks About*,[1] this very line was quoted and expounded in the context of the jealousy factor that had caused such a wrestling within Leah against her sister, understandably so. It struck me how much this applies to feelings of being invalidated as well.

Have you been dismissed as not good enough by certain standards, even though you yearned for validation and a stamp of approval? Next time the rejection of invalidation strikes, you can also say like Leah did, "This time, I will praise the Lord," and see what God will do with *that*! It will truly confuse the enemy![2] Furthermore, just imagine what all God can do when—instead of endlessly striving in our flesh to be validated, loved, accepted, or approved—we resign to worship Him in the midst of our dejected feelings of rejection, disappointment, and invalidation. It may feel contrary to our emotions at the time. However, by handling it this way, God's opportunity to intervene with favor on our behalf is exponentially increased. It cannot be overstated how great things happen when we worship Him, and all the more does He bless us when we do so while we're hurting. This is called a sacrifice of praise, which touches the heart of God to an incomparable degree!

When the fruit of Leah's lips praised God, it was from her praise that sprung forth which invoked God's validation of her to prove far better than Jacob's (or any earthly man's) validation of her could have been anyway. Little did she know that her suffering of invalidation was ultimately producing Kingdom purpose. The sons she birthed were Levi, of whom came the priesthood, and Judah, whose name means "praise," hence her infamous statement, "This time I will praise the Lord." As another significant note, it was from Judah's lineage that David, and most importantly, Jesus our Messiah came!

Lessons from Leah's invalidation from Jacob carry a striking resemblance to what we might experience in our modern days. Instead of pursuing those whose validation we crave, resorting to proving our worth and working in the flesh to win their approval and mark of recognition, we can be inspired by what Leah did when Judah was born. She finally quit trying to gain Jacob's affection and attention. She instead shifted her attention and hopes upon the Lord in praise of Him; as He was so much higher and worthy of honor anyway. Her blow of one more rejection evoked a new response: "This time I will praise the Lord."

From God's point of view, of course He does not rejoice at our suffering (although He can and does definitely use it to shape our character and ensure that we will also share in His glory). However, He was entirely pleased that Leah found His heart once she finally gave up trying to win Jacob's favor, since God wants to be the center of our deepest desire and affection anyway. His purposes in Leah were truly accomplished when her will was so bent that she no longer kept striving in the flesh for that which she was never able to attain. Rather, she fixed her eyes on the One Whose opinion mattered most.

This act of her will to worship instead of despair over the disillusionment and lack of fulfillment for earthly love and validation was precisely the miraculous, divine turning that God had been waiting to bless her with (and every generation thereafter). For it was out of her praise and affections toward God, as opposed to pursuing Jacob's attention or validation anymore, that resulted in the lineage of Jesus. It all began with the birth of her son, Judah, marking her pivotal turning to God—choosing to praise Him in place of her despair over Jacob's invalidation and lack of approval!

What God was wanting to see all along in Leah was not only for her attention to be on Him; but He wanted her desires to be for Him far above her desires for Jacob's affection, attention, and validation. This applies to us as well. He yearns for us to care far more about what He thinks and says of us, instead of what others think and say about us. He longs for us to set our gaze and affections on Him more than on what this world has to offer. In Colossians 3:1-3, we are told to set our minds on things above, where Christ is, because in all actuality, our lives are hidden with Christ in God. That is, our lives find their fulfillment in Him as He becomes our "All-in-all." He wants to be the highest, most sought after desire and source of affection in our lives such that people won't have such a strong hold on us as to feed or invalidate our sense of worth. Like with Leah, He has wanted to be the target of our deepest love, and as a natural overflow from this, giving us our sense of validation from our bond and holy union with Him. This is not because He is stingy and wants us to feel unloved in this world, but because He knows that His is the only Love that truly lasts and is stable, satisfies and fulfills, never comes up short, disappoints, or leaves us wanting.

Have you felt belittled or overshadowed by someone else's "bigger and better" story or status? Has it seemed like you have a drive within you to be heard or acknowledged—always competing against others to emerge as the validated one? Maybe this certain drive and longing within you is behind your suicide temptation, either because it seems like suicide is the only way to get your voice heard and your pain acknowledged; or because you are ready to give up the fight altogether as the feelings of invalidation are just too much to bear anymore. The truth is, both of those beliefs and pathways do end in utter exhaustion and hopelessness. There is a much, much better alternative.

The secret to overcoming anything in life—invalidation in terms of earth or other disappointments and pain—is to rise up with the soul fervor in declaring, "This time, I will praise the Lord," because there is literally no limit as to what God can do when we praise Him in place of our despair. Our worship of Him opens our lives to His infinite greatness and power in ways that even our most desperate pleadings in prayer won't, since worship magnifies Him in every glorious way; whereas wallowing in our desperation or pain keeps our attention on how big the problem or sorrow is within us. It is a matter of where our focus is (what we allow to be bigger in our eyes) that will determine our outcomes.

In one of my dark nights of the soul, Holy Spirit gave me a revelation along these lines. All I felt was pain. It was a season of sorrow for me in the most intense way I had ever known. Obviously I was fighting the temptation of suicide as a result of it. However, it was as if I was tapped on the shoulder in the night by the presence of God whispering what all the pain could become. The acronym for the word, "P-A-I-N" becomes **Praise Arising In Nighttime**. As contrary as it felt to my emotions to begin praising God in the midst of my pain, I realized it was exactly what Paul and Silas did when they were in prison. They simply praised God in their jail cell. Freedom came for them, because that is what praise does. We are the ones liberated as God is exalted. If you're wondering how this can possibly work, just try it. You will find out! As crazy as it may sound, next time your pain becomes so overwhelming that you start uttering words, "I want to die," turn your pain into **Praise Arising In Nighttime**. God responds every time to that. Why? Because God inhabits the praises of His people (Psalm 22:3).

A song that is old in years but timeless in truth can offer you a catchy way to remember the importance of our attention being set on Jesus instead of our pain when we have been invalidated by people or any other sorrow or struggle we are experiencing.

"When you're up against a struggle that shatters all your dreams
And your hopes have been cruelly crushed
by Satan's manifested schemes
And you feel the urge within you to submit to earthly fears
Don't let the faith you're standing in seem to disappear!

Praise the Lord, He can work through those who praise Him
Praise the Lord,
for our God inhabits praise.
Praise the Lord, for the chains that seem to bind you
Serve only to remind you that they drop powerless behind you
When you praise Him!

Now Satan is a liar and he wants to make us think
That we are paupers when he knows
himself we're children of the King.
So lift up the mighty shield of faith for the battle must be won
We know that Jesus Christ has risen so the work's already done!

Praise the Lord, He can work through those who praise Him
Praise the Lord, for our God inhabits praise.
Praise the Lord, for the chains that seem to bind you
Serve only to remind you that they drop powerless behind you
When you praise Him!…"[3]

One last thought to end this chapter on is to look at the way Jesus Himself handled the enemy's attempts of invalidating Him while He was on earth, dealing with harsh realities of life. In Isaiah 53:2, we're told that there was not anything about the appearance of Jesus that made Him stand out as particularly attractive. In other words, although He was the Son of God, He took on the garb of a servant. This is the description given in Philippians 2:5-8, "Your attitude should be the same as that of Christ Jesus: Who, being in very nature God, did not consider equality with God something to be grasped, but made Himself nothing, taking the very nature of a servant, being made in human likeness. And being found in appearance as a man, He humbled Himself and became obedient to death—even death on a cross!" Ironically, it goes on to say that because of this prized humility Jesus had, His Father exalted Him to the highest place. In essence, this can be true for us too in that we follow in Jesus' footsteps. As in Galatians 2:20, we have been crucified with Him, thus it is no longer we who live; we give up our rights to be validated and have any grounds for pride at all. Our humility will eventually lead to our promotion and validation by God, which is far superior than that which comes from our fellow man anyway.

Jesus is such an inspiring example to follow, because of all people who naturally had a right to carry an air about Him and demand validation and respect, He never did this. He was lowly, meek, and humble. Even so, it was a healthy self-concept that He had—never a victim mentality or a poor self-image. Those are mere counterfeits and not true humility or meekness at all! For instance, in John 11, where it's so famously quoted that Jesus wept, I've heard it argued that the entire reason for this was not because of grief and loss of Lazarus at all, as is the simplest implication. It's much deeper than that. His tears were about His sadness and angst over the people's unbelief; after all, He had claimed that Lazarus' life would not end in death. He knew He was going to be raising His friend from the dead. He was extremely secure in Who He was; His identity was healthy, strong, and solid. His grief was that the crowd did not believe Him, because as soon as Lazarus was dead, it was as if they completed invalidated Jesus' words.

So you see, Jesus definitely experienced the pain of being invalidated. Whether it was invalidation of Who He truly was (identity) or what He said (such powerful words as God-given authority in literally being and speaking the very Word), He was disbelieved and invalidated time after time. Along with this, He was even falsely accused as well. People mocked Him right at the time He was sacrificing His very life for the love of us all. In His darkest hour, cruel people were making fun of Him and kicking Him down further. Again, when was this? It was when He was giving Himself as a ransom for us—taking our punishments so we could escape eternal damnation. He was not only invalidated, but harshly ridiculed and scorned.

Yet what did our amazing example do? He kept His focus on His Father's approval and validation instead. He remained unmoved and unshaken by how people so casually dismissed and invalidated Him or His words, because He was utterly secure in His identity. He knew Who He was and Whom He served. He could entrust Himself to God Who ensures that honor will follow humility. Our Father's validation of us is all that matters; and my friend, that is something you already have if you're His child and submitted to Him! You don't have to strive to earn it; indeed you cannot. You already have His approval! Jesus obtained that for you!

Be encouraged—you are validated, heard, and dearly loved by the One Who never changes and by the One Whose opinion matters most and endures when all else fades away.

---

1 Kendall, RT. *Jealousy—The Sin No One Talks About: How To Overcome Envy & Live A Life of Freedom.* (Lake Mary, FL: Charisma House, 2010), 79.

2 Psalm 55:9

3 The Imperials. "Praise the Lord." Elliott B. Bannister/ Michael Vincent Hudson. *The Iconic Artists of Inspirational Music.* Warner/Chappell Music, Inc. http://www.songlyrics.com/the-imperials/praise-the-lord-lyrics/ Accessed December 26, 2020. (Punctuation added to lyrics for easier readability.)

GIVING AWAY OUR POWER

When life becomes so painful and overwhelming that we're ready to quit altogether, we typically feel powerless and utterly helpless. We become blind to how much power we actually do have, even if it might seem that we cannot do a single thing to change our circumstances. That is not where our power is found or measured in the first place. In Christ Jesus, we honestly are not powerless at all.

A close cousin of despair is a sense of powerlessness. It comes when our trust in God's goodness slips into doubt that He even cares at all; or that our fate might not have such a promising end after all. The enemy gains momentum once we bite on his bait of doubt, especially that which causes God's goodness to be in question.

Once we dip into the murky waters of doubt and unbelief, especially regarding God's character or that our future holds any hope, we easily transfer a sense of powerlessness to people or even situations. We lose our sure footing of remembering that God is our Rock, our Stronghold and High Tower. Psalm 62:11 says, "All power belongs to God." This is to our comfort, not our dismay! Why? Because He gives us His power as our inheritance; this is part of our identity in Christ. We have been made joint heirs with Jesus. So, everything God the Father has given Jesus is shared with us too. We are even seated with Jesus in heavenly places.[1] Thus, it is only the enemy's lies that convince us that we are powerless or helpless.

Furthermore, Jeremiah 29:11 tells us that God has thoughts and plans for us that are full of hope and peace in our final outcome, not evil. Again, it's when we entertain doubt about this that our healthy sense of power evaporates. In fact, we often "give away our power" to other people without realizing it. Since this is a subtle way despair sets in and gets such a stranglehold on us as to bring on suicide temptation, this chapter serves to expose the roots of the powerless problem and the solution.

Have you ever felt controlled by someone or circumstances as if you had no say-so at all? I lived a great number of years in this controlling predicament. Not only did it breed a spirit of control in my own life—whereby I exerted an unhealthy sense of control; but it all became a cyclical illusion anyway. I became increasingly *out* of control, which caused a domino effect of other problems. I struggled to let go in relationships, just as I had difficulty relinquishing control over things in my own personal life and behaviors that kept me so bound, as if locked in an internal prison.

A wise counselor finally asked me one day, "Why do you give away your power?" Her statement struck a chord in me, yet I was immediately defensive. Over time, however, the truth and reality of her point hit home to my heart as my eyes were opened. I really was the one allowing others (or circumstances) to control me by giving away the power that should have been rightfully mine. For example, I allowed what they thought of me to dominate my actions or words. I let their opinions about my life sway and determine my decisions.

In fact, this was such a deeply rooted behavior pattern that had been ingrained into my very personality at a young age. During my teen years, an adult in a stepmother role of sorts (not a biological family member) who spent considerable time with me heavily influenced me from her own dysfunctional, unhealthy mental and emotional state. She had a certain spiritual darkness about her as well, which defied the One True God. Obviously, at the vulnerable age and situation I was in, I was unaware of the extent of just how wrong this was, as my own personality took such gradual shifts into melancholy and darkened change under her extremely controlling ways. Only later, with a counselor's help, was I able to see that there was actually lots of emotional and spiritual abuse going on, to the point that my own identity became so confused and lost altogether. The best description I can give of what happened to my mind was like someone taking a deck of cards from a person, reshuffling them, so that the person no longer knows what they have anymore. Even as a young adult in my twenties, although I had moved away from their home in which I lived for a number of years, I no longer knew what I personally thought or felt about anything. It would be an understatement to say that an extreme brainwashing had taken place. I merely lived on autopilot in terms of what this lady had imposed into my mind with her own thoughts, beliefs, and feelings in a mind-controlling way. I even somehow took on her personality as my own, as if I had become a clone and my very soul had been prostituted. Having lived those earlier years under the repeated shaming and condemning, passive-aggressive punishing ways for expressing my own identity, personality, thoughts, and feelings, I was enslaved in assuming her identity as my own in order to gain her acceptance and love, which was never achieved. My own family later described it as if the Glena they knew had died and had become someone else.

It took many years to untangle from this. It was like a house showing the symptoms of a cracked foundation after years of subtle damage taking place beneath the surface. My precious heritage and roots of Christian upbringing had been mocked by her bitterness for so long that I went through a period of intense confusion about God's character. Of course, this slip-and-slide of doubting His love, goodness, and overall truth found in His Word wreaked havoc with my mental, emotional, and spiritual stability. This caused a vast array of problems which shattered my soul on many levels. The fragmentation of my mind, my belief system in relating to God, the confining imprisonment and greying-out of my personality, and more were all deeply damaged areas that needed to be healed, delivered, restored, and rebuilt by truth to replace all the lies and evil sway.

Moreover, I had learned so well to live out this other person's thoughts, feelings, personality, and behavior instead of my own that I simply transferred this pattern to every other relationship I had as a deeply driven hunger for approval, love, and acceptance. Drawing from my own experience as an illustration, this is how and where it comes into play about giving away our power. Again, it was a lengthy process of counseling and recovery to learn how to break this habitual cycle and claim my own identity and healthy sense of control, beginning with ownership of my own thoughts, feelings, personality, and decisions, regardless of others' opinions. God's love was the empowering factor, as I finally learned that His love never fails, fades, or changes. Again, because "all power belongs to God," He imputes that into us as His dearly beloved ones. If you feel powerless like I once did, let God's love empower you to embrace your true identity in Christ; herein lies your hope!

My purpose in sharing this brief background is to let you know that I do understand what it's like to be controlled by someone in a literal, manipulative, and punitive sense—whether it is to an abusive degree, or in milder ways that are nonetheless still valid. By the same token, I also understand firsthand how difficult it is to untangle your personhood from the messy web of sticky, controlling relationships or situations. Even physically, it can be extremely hard to break free from an abusive relationship. I went to the drastic measure of moving out of state in my early twenties just to get out of that very predicament, so I do relate if this is where you are.

Yet while you hear my heart of compassion and understanding, be encouraged to see that you can indeed break free from controlling powers and live a mentally, emotionally healthy life such that you exercise control of your own life in proper ways. Letting others dictate and determine our course is what happens when despair yields that desperately helpless feeling; but we do have a voice and will continue to have one as long as we're still breathing! It's when we give up even this (our very breath, by our own will) that we lose.

In fact, as powerless as you might feel in this pressing, painful situation that has you convinced that the only way to cope is to end your life, consider the idea that the one power we do have is to choose life. In spite of how helpless we may feel in our current situations, the words of Jesus proclaim that we have more power than we may realize. In Acts 1:8, He says that when the Holy Spirit comes upon us, we will receive power, and will be able to tell others the Good News. This was said in context of Jesus speaking to His disciples just before ascending to heaven, imploring and admonishing them to spread the hope of redemption that His death and resurrection promises. So all the more, can you even begin to fathom the passionate cry of the Lord to you in your position now—bowed low with pressing hardship and struggles to find hope? He would surely say to you as He did to them, in essence, "I am giving you the Holy Spirit to be your source of power and ability—not only to come through this with a living hope; but then to tell others how you made it. How your life found new hope and a sense of power after all—in Me, that the grave could not conquer Me; therefore, it will not conquer you either."

Another encouragement from Jesus that you really have been given power, no matter how defeated and powerless you may see yourself, is given in His own words. He says, "Behold, I have given you authority and *power*...and [physical and mental strength and ability] over all the power that the enemy [possesses]; and *nothing* shall in any way harm you" (Luke 10:19 AMPC; italics mine). In my own personal experience, powerlessness was one of the driving forces behind my ever-pressing temptation to end it all. For many years, I continually felt that I had no control over anything in my life. In fact, through a desperately difficult battle with an eating disorder that all but completely ruined my health, I found my addictive ways and attempts at control to be my only "say-so," which obviously proved how out of control I actually was! It took a very long time to realize and truly live out the hope given here in the Lord's words to us. He has not only given us a healthy power and authority to exercise in our lives, but even a power and authority to overcome that which the enemy attempts to exert over us. What the enemy meant for our harm, God can turn for our good.[2]

Because of this, let's determine to run the race with a renewed sense of empowerment and authority instead of succumbing to that darkly closed-in, powerless feeling of "no way out." We cannot afford to give away our power as if we have no worth. After all, Jesus was giving us this high call and responsibility as ones who could go into all the world as representatives of Him, to others who are downtrodden, hurting, and deeply broken as we have been ourselves. As you seek hope, you will have the opportunity to pass it on to others later. This may not be of much comfort right now, hurting to the depths as you might be. However, if you can somehow get a picture of someone else in mind who might be in the exact position and situation as you are now, imagine the reward of realizing you did not give away your power by yielding to the temptation of suicide, which would be letting the enemy win and have all the power. That day will come, if you don't give up now, when your life story will give someone hope. It's just the way God's Kingdom works!

Granted, there may not be much we can do in the way of damage that has already been done in our past—to ourselves or to others; and many aspects of our situation may indeed be irreversible. Nevertheless, insofar as we utilize our God-given sense of power and authority, rather than merely throwing it away, new opportunities of redemption can and will surely follow. There is light at the end of this long, dark tunnel. We simply can't let the cross of Jesus Christ, and all the torturous pain He endured for us, be in vain. We must keep reaching for the hope that we are promised in Him; for He says that those who keep asking will receive, those who keep seeking will surely find, and for those who keep knocking, the door will be opened.[3] It may be that the one remaining "say-so" we have left is the choice to live, which is powerful in itself! Truly, although we can't undo the past, our one most powerful choice of living can even provide a redemptive opportunity to see new doors open that can allow our hearts some mending, as we let God do His creative art of restoration, which would be permanently cut off if we had chosen to take a willful exit too soon.

Let's choose life, aspiring to having no more regrets, and see what the forward adventure holds in store. Jesus' resurrection power can be ours too, as we endeavor to pour newfound energy into the hope of our redemption story. It is so possible that new doors are right on the brink of opening that we never thought possible. God does promise that nothing is impossible with Him.[4] Faith is key. We can tap into a reservoir of hope if only we will not give up too soon, and importantly look to Jesus for that hope, and not to our surroundings, circumstances, other people, and other earthly means for hope, which will inevitably disappoint. God is worth our wait. Psalm 30:5 (AMPC) says, "Weeping may endure for a night, but joy comes in the morning." If this were not true, it would not be in the Word of God; and His Word never returns void, empty, or useless without producing the effect or purpose for which it was sent.[5] We can stake our entire lives on what the Bible says, as we seek hope from it; because God is not a God that He should lie, and His Word absolutely never fails.[6]

---

1 Ephesians 2:6
2 Genesis 50:20
3 Luke 11:9
4 Luke 1:37
5 Isaiah 55:11
6 Numbers 23:19

TRACING THE "T THEME"

This book by no means offers a conclusive account of suicide prevention, including the causes behind the struggle. However, grounded in personal experience, it has been in retracing my own steps through this certain battle of contemplating suicide, and listening to others share their perspectives too, that I have found what I will call a "T theme." This chapter breaks down various points that may trace not only the source cause of our dilemma, but also traces the steps beyond it that are available to us—all beginning with a "T" as a point of reference in mapping your journey from despair to hope.

Before we begin, please note, you will frequently find the words, "But God" in quotation marks. I would love to give credit to whom it is due, yet honestly do not know who originally made this such a popular phrase to convey the power of God. In this context, it is meant to express how a seemingly hopeless situation gives way to the exception of God stepping into it, thus changing everything.

"Trapped" in our situation is obviously how we are feeling in some way to be convinced that suicide is the only solution. So many times, it is a piling up of painful issues, problems, or occurrences that have built up within us over time. Our innate "fight or flight" instinct has, however effectively, recruited the very last of our reserves until our manageability of it all begins to collapse altogether, sometimes by only a slight trigger. We reach the proverbial "last straw" when it feels like all of life is caving in on us, leaving us very overwhelmed, and at a loss of how to cope. Yet, we are also, no doubt, in too deep to see things objectively. This is when we need to draw on sources beyond ourselves; because it's the enemy not only lying to us that we are trapped, but he is convincing us that we know best, which is absolutely false. Although this may sound oversimplified as common sense, it really is helpful and wise to seek counsel either professionally, or at least with a trusted person. If you have no one like this, pray that God will provide someone. This is a prayer He would love to answer, since it is what His Word says to do.[1] Feeling trapped is one thing; but choosing to feel trapped by yourself is unnecessary. Yes, taking the risk to open your heart is a huge one. Notwithstanding, this just may prove to be one of the first ways you experience God's help and healing. He will not only meet you where you are, but will carry you much further than you could ever manage to go on your own. Plus, He blesses and honors your humility in this way. Begin here by asking Him to supply you with the specific courage needed in reaching out to someone trustworthy.

Satan is not creative at all. In fact, he cannot even "create" anything. He can only use and expound on what responses we give him when he attacks us. Therefore, know that the hopelessness of feeling trapped is such a bold lie from the realm of darkness, because the Word is full of stories in which people felt this same way by the enemy's set up in their lives; "but God" came through for them in some memorably victorious way when they gave Him the gift of their belief.

Job must have felt trapped in despair, considering his sequence of catastrophic losses. He was so depressed by feeling trapped in his own suffering that he cursed the day of his birth, and wanted to die.[2] "But God" came through for him when Job finally found peace in acknowledging God's sovereignty.[3] Furthermore, God restored his life to greater joy in what he gained later, which compensated for all his former losses and suffering.[4] Although Job never could see hope coming, and felt crushing despair and grief at the time he felt so trapped by suffering, God's plan all along was to recompense and restore him to a life that was better than what he had prior to all the pain. If Job had taken his own life, he would have aborted this possibility of God's reward awaiting him on the other side of his severe trials and testing.

Opposite of our enemy, God is the ultimate Creator with the special name of *Elohim*. He can create stunning beauty from the ugliest ashes of ruin and loss. He has been fulfilling this promise of His for centuries, and continues to this day![5] God can restore that which has been broken, lost, or destroyed in some creative way, but only if we give Him a chance by asking, along with the patient waiting of time for Him to do it!

Others in Biblical history also experienced the desire to die that must have come from feeling trapped, "but God" answered when they chose faith over feelings. Elijah, who the Bible reports as being "a person just like us" was another who expressed a desire for his life to end, because he was feeling trapped by depression and fear.[6] "But God" came through for him by sending an angel to minister to his physical need of nourishment, his emotional need of encouragement, and his spiritual need of renewed purpose.

Solomon felt trapped by an empty life, once he reached the height of having acquired riches, pleasure, and success, only to find out how unfulfilling and useless it all was in the end. He reached a point of hating his life.[7] "But God" taught him how to tap into a much higher, more fulfilling purpose of reverencing his God, loving His Word, and obeying His commands.[8]

Jonah felt trapped by God's call upon his life, and became so depressed as a result of his own disobedience to where God wanted him to go. When he finally repented and accepted his God-given second chance, the Lord was able to accomplish great results in Ninevah through him. Although his attitude was by no means a perfect model, even after his missionary work was completed, God illustrates through this book of Jonah how His prevailing heart of compassion and mercy always triumphs over judgment.[9] He loved not only the people of Ninevah too much to let Jonah dismiss God's call on his life; but He also loved Jonah too much to let him get away with an embittered spirit, which we are able to see firsthand always leads to destruction.

From the New Testament, Paul serves as another great example in suffering and feeling trapped from all angles as he vulnerably shares how he felt. "For we were so utterly burdened beyond our strength that we despaired of life itself" (II Corinthians 1:8 ESV). "We were hedged in (pressed) on every side [troubled and oppressed in every way], but not cramped or crushed; we suffer embarrassments and are perplexed and unable to find a way out, but not driven to despair. We are pursued (persecuted and hard driven), but not deserted [to stand alone]; we are struck down to the ground, but never struck out and destroyed" (II Corinthians 4:8-9 AMP).[10]

What is incredibly remarkable and outstanding about Paul's honest admittance in how he and his group felt is that he actually uses these descriptions to draw out an important, winning truth that demonstrates the saving "but God" exception best of all. That is, he recognized the opportunity to make an all-important shift with his focus. Despite his overwhelming hardships, he still realized that his frail human life, a mere earthen vessel, contained the "precious treasure" of eternal hope and salvation offered in Jesus. Therefore, he was motivated to persevere so that "the grandeur and exceeding greatness of the power may be shown to be from God and not from ourselves" (II Corinthians 4:7 AMP).

Notice the humility as well as where He places his hope in another statement he made. "Indeed, we felt within ourselves that we had received the very sentence of death, but that was to keep us from trusting in and depending on ourselves instead of on God Who raises the dead. For it is He Who rescued and saved us from such a perilous death, and He will still rescue and save us; in and on Him we have set our hope (our joyful and confident expectation) that He will again deliver us from danger and destruction and draw us to Himself" (II Corinthians 1:9-10 AMPC).

Finally, he trumps the best inspiration of what to do in our times of feeling trapped by such pressing difficulties that hedge us in so severely, as he described in his own experience. That is, as he expresses such extreme hardship, he essentially always ends with "but God" encouraged and comforted us, so that we could, in turn, encourage and comfort others. In essence, he is saying that regardless of all the ways they were trapped by suffering, such that they thought they were going to die, the Lord came through for them with such a prevailing sense of strength, comfort, encouragement, and hope that they not only survived; but they became empowered to give back to others all that they had received from God themselves. They allowed God's tool of adversity to fill them with such compassion and empathy for others who were suffering that they discovered great purpose in seeing God's power at work and flowing through their lives! In this way, the enemy became trapped in his own snare, instead of his attempted trap of God's servants in which he intended to extinguish their lives altogether! We can follow this same pattern for helping others when we allow the severity of pain to trap our lying enemy, and in turn, start showing others who are hurting that we do understand what it is to hurt to the Nth degree; "but God" can offer a comfort and hope like no other when we let Him use it all for His glory.

An excellent modern day example of this is Joni Eareckson Tada. Personally, I so appreciate the honesty in her life story following her diving accident, when she became a quadriplegic. She admitted how much she wanted to die when it first happened, as she obviously felt trapped in her own paralyzed body that would be stuck in a wheelchair for life.[11] "But God" was lovingly fighting for her best interest in His heart. To witness her life now, one cannot help but see Jesus. She has become a living trophy of His grace in every way. Ever so dramatically, God has transformed her mental attitude from despair to hope. Furthermore, He has changed her heart from that former place of intense struggle with depression when she was first disabled to a richly fulfilling intimacy with Him, which now naturally overflows in her ability to minister worldwide to others with disabilities. In fact, her life is being so powerfully infused with God's purpose in that she can even minister to those without disabilities too—all because we easily see Jesus through her beautiful zest for living even from a wheelchair! Drawing the perfect illustration of how this is possible is the following truth.

> "Grace (favor and spiritual blessing) to you and heart peace from God our Father and the Lord Jesus Christ (the Messiah, the Anointed One).
>
> Blessed be the God and Father of our Lord Jesus Christ, the Father of sympathy (pity and mercy) and the God Who is the Source of every comfort (consolation and encouragement).
>
> Who comforts…us in every trouble (calamity and affliction), so that we may also be able to comfort…those who are in any kind of trouble or distress, with the comfort…with which we ourselves are comforted…by God.
>
> For just as Christ's own sufferings fall to our lot as they overflow upon His disciples, and we share and experience them abundantly, so through Christ's comfort…is also shared and experienced abundantly by us.
>
> But if we are troubled (afflicted and distressed), it is for your comfort…and for your salvation; and if we are comforted…it is for your comfort…which works in you when you patiently endure the same evils (misfortunes and calamities) that we also suffer and undergo" (II Corinthians 1:2-6 AMP).

Conversely, there were those in the Bible who felt too trapped that they took matters in their own hands. As you read their contrasted outcomes, it becomes obvious that they lost a great victory by forfeiting their faith in God being the one powerful antidote to their despair. Whatever they were facing, they ended their own situations with a permanent period at their own handmade end, instead of leaving room for a "but God" exception, whereby the Lord would have definitely responded if He had been given a chance.

"Temptation," therefore, is one of the main underlying components along this T theme. Suicide must be one of the enemy's favorite kinds of temptation of all, since it not only so boldly defies the sovereignty and Life-giving power of God; but as John 10:10 tells us, "The enemy comes to steal, kill, and destroy." Of course, his main objective is theft and destruction of a life that God deems as "precious" and "chosen."[12] To give into the temptation of suicide is to become merely another statistic—and even worse, another Judas in some ways—which is exactly what the enemy wants. Consistent with his lying, scheming ways of darkness, Satan's plot behind his tempting us with suicide is to force us into the ultimate betrayal of our Lord, Who gave His absolute *all* in order that we would be spared the eternal death penalty by receiving Jesus' gift of everlasting life.

How differently Judas' story could have ended, if only he could have known that the very Blood being shed for him within hours of those fatal moments he chose to punish himself by suicide was a Price that could have forgiven, redeemed, and set him free. He was within moments of God's only Son paying the highest cost for *his* life, for *his* ransom. That is, in the very hour of hanging himself from all the guilt, shame, and betrayal for which he was punishing himself, Jesus was actually taking his punishment upon His own body instead. Hope could have been his once again; but he gave up too soon, which must have been an even greater insult than all the mockery that was verbally shouted at Jesus while He was dying a cruel death for us on the Cross.

"Terrified" also follows the T theme as a common tool the enemy uses in tempting us with suicide's seemingly easy way out. This was my own stronghold for many years indeed. I had been traumatized, which had a generalized way of enslaving me to fear for quite some time, since the enemy had gotten such a foothold in my life through this opened door. In other words, fear can be a powerfully driving force in the mind, pushing us to unhealthy extremes of bondage; but it's only allowed to go so far as we yield to it. Otherwise stated, fear only has power over us when we let it have control. It took me years of learning this the hard way until I finally understood how much ground I was giving the enemy to torment me with fear. No wonder I lived as such a victim, feeling utterly helpless and powerless in almost every area of my life. It was as if the breaker box of my mind, so to speak, was tripped during a storm; and thereafter, my mental default setting typically reverted to suicidal thoughts as a way to escape being so afraid.

The Word says it best how that fear really does have torment. I lived in such a tormenting grip myself to testify how true this is. What dynamic makes this interesting, however, is that the antidote to fear is God's perfect love. One may ask, "How can it be that easy?" This was my own question for so long that remained an unanswered mystery until I began experiencing fresh revelations of God's quality of perfect love. It is a love like no other source. His is a perfect, matchless, unconditional kind of love that far surpasses mere human experience on earth. If you have been wounded and the idea of being unconditionally loved eludes you, know that God's love for you never fails; for it is of a much higher quality that will not leave you hurting, forsaken, or disappointed. Ask Him with an open heart, eyes, and ears to receive fresh revelations of His love. This is a hunger and thirst He loves to fill, because it is the essence of Who He is. Love is definitely a covenant word, and "God is love…" (I John 4:8). He has made a covenant of love with you. Therefore, His responses will certainly begin setting you free by the truth and reality of His perfect love.

Here is a promise from His own Word of how fear and love compete as virtual opposites, presenting our problem (of being terrified and tormented by fear), and His solution (of perfect love casting out our fear and utterly removing our sense of dread, punishment, or pending harm). "There is no fear in love [dread does not exist]. But perfect (complete, full-grown love) drives out fear, because fear involves…punishment, so the one who is afraid…is not perfected in love [has not grown into sufficient understanding of God's love]" (I John 4:18 AMP).

As basic as the subject of God's love may seem, we really never outgrow our need for further growth, receptivity, and understanding of His love; but rather, are encouraged to experience it to deeper, higher, and richer measure. This enables us to experience the fullness of God's presence, even during painful times, as it is His love that will naturally heal and deliver us from the torment of fear, anxiety, traumatic effects, and every other source of despair that causes us to lose our will to live. This following passage expresses the power that is available to us in God's love.

> "May He grant you out of the riches of His glory, to be strengthened and spiritually energized with power through His Holy Spirit in your inner self, [indwelling your innermost being and personality] so that Christ may dwell in your hearts through your faith.
>
> And may you, having been deeply rooted and securely grounded in love, be fully capable of comprehending with all…God's people, the width and length and height and depth of His love [fully experiencing that amazing, endless love]; and that you may come to know practically, through personal experience, the love of Christ which far surpasses mere knowledge without experience, that you may be filled up throughout your being to all the fullness of God [so that you may have the richest experience of God's presence in your lives, completely filled and flooded with God Himself].
>
> Now to Him Who is able to carry out His purpose and do superabundantly more than all that we dare ask or think [infinitely beyond our greatest prayers, hopes, or dreams], according to His power that is at work within us…" (Ephesians 3:16-20 AMP).[13]

In summary, we are only feeling powerless and terrified when we are allowing such fear to control us. The enemy is like a roaring lion; he is always seeking someone to devour.[14] Remember though, he is just a toothless lion at best! Don't let him threaten you into such a tiny pinhole escape by way of suicide, just to silence his roar! If you can picture that it is only a loud sound he makes, take courage by silencing him with music of your own, namely that will exalt Who Jesus is, through praise and worship. You will be astounded at the results this yields, as you will not only feel less afraid—(remembering how perfect love casts out fear, and when we worship, we invite God's presence of perfect love into our hearts); but we will also find the enemy's threats of intimidation fade and lessen. We are promised that we are held in the palm of God's hands, and no one can pluck us out of His hands.[15] However, when we give into the enemy's intimidating threats of fear by taking our own lives, we are playing God's role; and this is dangerous territory! Beautifully described in the above passage, we are offered a better alternative for how to live. The answer to overcoming fear-based captivity is found in God's love, where His promises circle around our protection. The solution is not in committing suicide.

Tracing the T theme to the answers that hold our hope involve two words: "Trust" and "Through." In all of these tight places wherein you find yourself squeezed by suicidal temptation—feeling trapped, tempted by total despair, terrified or traumatized—it all leads to one hopeful alternative of trusting God. Before you scoff at the simplistic sound of this, understand that before you were ever formed in your mother's womb, your days were planned, ordained, numbered, and established by your Creator. Please read Psalm 139 to see what God saw and knew as you were being created in His hands. Also, hear this from God's heart regarding your life, "'For I know the plans and thoughts that I have for you,' says the Lord, 'plans for peace and well-being and not for disaster, to give you a future and a hope'" (Jeremiah 29:11 AMP). If we will trust Him at His Word on these plans of His that we cannot feel or see, we will eventually realize this promised future and hope; yet if we take matters into our own hands by ending it all on our own time and plans, "disaster" will indeed be the result of aborting Almighty God's plans for our lives.

Interestingly, when God spoke this powerful Word to His people, they were exiled in Babylonian captivity; and life was not going well for them at all. Their future looked bleak; they felt ruined and in despair, as one might describe. God spoke this as a drawing of their hearts to trust Him, that He would bring them forward to better days of hope. Would they trust Him? As these words are spoken to us now, will *we* trust Him?

Chances are, for the wounds you may carry, trust has been a badly damaged ability of yours. It was for me also. However, one of the first endearing ways of loving us that God seeks to mend is our realization that He is utterly trustworthy. As we experience this character quality of our Heavenly Father, our ability to trust Him is naturally healed and strengthened over time. Initially though, we simply have to take the risk and dare to trust Him, based on what He has promised in His Word. Hebrews 13:5-6 (AMP) assures us that He will never leave us or forsake us, or even relax His hold on us! Therefore, we need not live in fear or give way to despair. God is truly for us. In fact, Isaiah 30:18 (AMP) shows us that He is actually longing with eagerness to shine His favor on us, meaning that He is waiting for us to trust and expect Him to help us; and certainly, He will meet us where we are at every point of our need. He is looking to be gracious to us, and loves it when we deposit our trust in Him to do so.

What really gave me hope and helped me during my times of temptation to give up was a revelation He showed me on the word, "Through," which is the last part of this T theme that ends with hope! It began in Psalm 77:19 (AMP) where it says that He delivered His people, "but His footsteps were obliterated." We may not always know when, how, or where God will come through for us, but if He led His people *through* the Red Sea, the wilderness, imprisonment, and more, He is a trustworthy God Who will see us through our desperation too, never abandoning us midway. The trail God blazes *through* a situation may be so creative that we don't even know about it. Be open to God's quality of creativity. It may be that an unforeseen, entirely new season in your life awaits. Don't abort the possibilities! God can create beauty from ashes and joy from mourning. In fact, He can create stunning array out of absolute nothingness and dark void, as in the very beginning of creation. He can take messes and make majestic outcomes. He only asks that we be still and know that He is God as we wait on Him to lead us "through" our struggles, by accomplishing in our lives all that is in His heart.[16]

"Through" is the key operative word that makes the shift from the ominous question of "How will I make it?" The answer is through Jesus. Hebrews 12:1-2 says that He is the Author and Finisher of our faith; thus, we must keep our gaze fixed on Him the entire way of our journey, no matter the struggles we encounter. One step at a time, you will come *through* this fire of affliction or difficult season of your life; but it cannot be in our own strength. It is through Jesus, specifically, that we find victory and strength to persevere and ultimately win. Philippians 4:13 assures us how we can find the adequate strength we need: "I can do all things *through* Christ, Who infuses inner strength into me." Moreover, we are promised, "We overcome by the blood of the Lamb and the word of our testimony" (Revelation 12:11). That is, *through* the blood of Jesus, acknowledging how He has helped us through each and every challenge, progressively allowing this to build within us a heart of praise and gratitude, we find ourselves overcoming the despair that once held us captive.

1 Galatians 6:2, James 5:16

2 Job 3:11, 6:9

3 Job 38:1-5, 40:1-4

4 Job 42:12-14

5 Isa 61:1-3

6 I Kings 19:1-18; James 5:17

7 Ecclesiastes 2:17

8 Ecclesiastes 12:13

9 James 2:13

10 This passage was made present tense by the author for consistency

11 Tada, Joni Eareckson; Musser, Joe. *Joni: An Unforgettable Story.* (Grand Rapids, MI: Zondervan Publishing Company, 1977).

12 Isaiah 43:4, Ephesians 1:4

13 Punctuation altered by author for easier readability

14 I Peter 5:8

15 John 10:28-29

16 Psalm 46:10

DEATH OF A DIFFERENT KIND

Slow suicide is still suicide. Are you slowly destroying yourself as a more subtle way of suicide to ease your conscience? Maybe you're assuming you are hurting your loved ones less, or not so much at all this way, as opposed to a more deliberate, instantaneous attempt. This was my false belief and lifestyle for many years, which is why it has been so heavily on my heart to write a book for others being pressured by the same despair that slowly erodes hope.

On the one hand, I feared God too much to make a drastic, swift and sudden attempt at ending my own life; while on the other hand, my battle primarily involved such a strong sense of guilt and shame that I felt like abusing myself in deliberate, but slow self-destruction was more of my deserved style of punishment anyway. This thought process, albeit deceptive, lessened my overburdened conscience, since I felt like I wasn't hurting anyone else as a fatally quick incidence in one day would. Indeed, I was quite deceived. Family and friends were still deeply hurt, because slow, subtle suicide is just the same as the one event kind. Satan is a master deceiver; he will always sugar-coat lies and feed them to us on a tasty spoonful, convincing us all the while that we are justified in our own ways.

For well over twenty years, I struggled relentlessly with anorexia and bulimia, always knowing in the deepest core of my soul that the addictive restlessness within me driving me to such madness was all about punishing myself, even more so than it being about body image, control issues, or other factors. Self-starvation attempts represented such a hopelessness within me about my life in general, while also punishing myself for the heavy guilt and shame I carried for so long, and believing that I did not deserve to live at all, let alone enjoy my life. A hot cauldron of self-hatred boiled within me, fueled by the many lies I was believing. When various circumstances would trigger me, I took it out on myself rather harshly as a means of hastening my death, as if gasoline was poured onto the fires already burning within me.

Despite the healing that did come ever so gradually in my heart and spirit first—long before my addictive behavior, mindset, and physical being ever showed a hint of change—it was the co-existing battle with severe depression that was even stronger, which is also what kept repeatedly tempting me with suicide being my only way out. Here again, having walked the journey of intense despair to hope, and knowing what all God has worked out in me over the years, has filled me with so much compassion for others who are experiencing the same blinding, pressuring temptation of wanting so desperately to end it all that it seems like there is no other alternative, certainly no more hope to be had. I have been there. It hurts beyond description. In fact, a temptation of suicide is often considered too shameful to mention at all within the church or in Christian circles especially; because a higher standard is expected—even of one's struggles!

Therefore, one of the first foundational truths I encountered and had to embrace has been the fact that Jesus condemns absolutely no one. When the woman caught in the very act of adultery was brought to Jesus—in front of a crowd of judgmental gossipers and condemning onlookers—His gentle answer was that He did not condemn her! Hear the same being spoken to you in your tears. He certainly does not condemn you either in your struggle with this, or with anything else for that matter. Your secrets and struggles are not only safe with Him, but He can help like no one else can. You are *always* welcome to reach out to Him even at 3 a.m. when no one else would appreciate that; He actually does! He's watching over you at all hours day and night anyway, ready and available for you anytime.

In fact, what has drawn me to Jesus in this certain struggle is the picture of Him in the Garden of Gethsemane when He was so desperate and in emotional pain just prior to being crucified that He pleaded with the Father for that cup of suffering to pass from Him. To us, our cup of suffering might be to live, when all within us is writhing in emotional (and possibly physical) pain desperately wanting to die, longing that the cup of suffering pass from us too. I have repeatedly drawn strength and inspiration from the next words He spoke, however. He said, "Nevertheless, not my will; but Your will be done." Ironically, in His case, to accept the cup was to submit to death; while in our case, to submit is to live. Make no mistake, Jesus understands the pain of such pressure; in fact, His desperation was so intense as He cried out to God in prayer that He actually sweated drops of blood.

As you grow in the Word and in your journey of knowing Jesus better, you will find that we are actually called to die to ourselves—our flesh. This is not referring to a physical death. It is a putting to death of all our fleshly ways: "dying to self." What does this mean exactly? We have been crucified with Christ. It is no longer possible to have it both ways—living for self or living for Jesus. We must choose to deny ourselves, take up our cross, and follow Him. As the best Teacher Who ever lived by example, Jesus is not asking us to do anything He did not already do Himself. Again, it may not look the same exactly. He submitted to dying on the Cross so we would not have to go through that degree of torture. But the death He does call us to is an extinguishing of all our self-driven ways—the sins that easily entangle us, the lusts of our flesh, such as greed, idolatry, or just insisting on our own ways based on selfish human tendencies. His Word expresses this concept the best: "My old self has been crucified with Christ. It is no longer I who live, but Christ lives in me. So I live in this earthly body by trusting in the Son of God, Who loved me and gave Himself for me" (Galatians 2:20 NLT).

Deeply internalize the agony and torture that Jesus suffered on the Cross because of how much He loves you—how He gave up all of Himself and all He had of His royalty in heaven, how He chose to humble Himself by becoming human on earth, with the ability to feel all our pain and experience death for us. Consider what an incredibly high price He placed on your life to do this for you. Let this soak into your heart and soul for a while.

Then think about what your plan of suicide does to His heart. Is it not the ultimate cruelty of throwing it all back in His face? You see, you were bought with a price—the highest one of all, the Blood of Jesus, God's only Son. There was literally no greater sacrifice than this, that He laid down His life for you, even while you were still a sinner.[1] As painful as your situation must be, understand that *because* you were bought with such a high price, you really are not your own.[2] You belong to the One Who loves you infinitely greater than anyone else ever could. As you meditate on this degree of love and depth of ownership, responsibility, and personal investment He has in your life by His own Bloodshed, the temptation to commit suicide has to lose its power. Love conquers all; love is greater than fear, pain, rage, betrayal, rejection, abandonment, and failure. See, when we die to the "self-life," including all the pain and worldly distress that goes along with it, we become alive unto God. We can live in a delivered state from the despair of suicide just by remembering our old nature has died with Christ. Our sin is rendered powerless and completely atoned for; we don't have to continue living as slaves to sin anymore.[3] We are made new creations in Jesus. The old has passed away, and behold, all things become new.[4] "I belong to my Beloved, and His desire is for me" (Song of Solomon 7:10 NIV).

Paul said, "For me, to live is Christ, and to die is gain" (Philippians 1:21 NKJV). He understood with great anticipatory joy that this world was not his true home, heaven was. However, in dying to himself—his own desires and wishes, he realized that there was a more important, higher work for him to engage in that required him to remain in this broken, pain-filled world. He accepted the call to endure whatever injustices and hardships might be part of his journey while on earth; because his heartbeat was to respond to the higher calling of spreading the Good News of salvation to others, no matter the opposition.

When we are so blinded by emotional or physical pain, or mental turmoil and pressure, it can be extremely difficult to rise above our own "world" to gain this higher, more other-focused view. Yet this has the potential to help not only set us free from our own tight place of bondage and suffering, but also provides a catalyst for turning our perspective more outward, rather than inward all the time. Pain of any kind has such a strong way of keeping us self-absorbed, and even justifiably so, we might argue! For example, our insides might be screaming, "If the pain *wasn't* so intensely unbearable, then surely I *could* think of someone or something else for a change; but it is ever burning and present 24/7!" Interestingly, the nature, character, and Word of God suggests that this works in reverse of what we might be tempted to think and feel. Joel Osteen is famous for saying, "What we make happen for someone else, God will make happen for you." If you want to go deeper, here is a passage from what God has spoken Himself.

At first glance, this may seem out of context, as this is talking about God's true heart's desire for us when we fast; but there is a striking parallel, since we are, after all, talking about denying ourselves (our selfish will and appetite of wanting our own way). The context here is God expressing His disdain for mere mechanical fasting—going through the external "motions of penance" while being inwardly puffed up in pride, having no genuine softening heart value at all. Instead, what He loves is our authentic humility and doing for others what they cannot do for themselves. The key that brings this home to make my point is His beautiful illustration of what happens when we do this. Listen to how God describes what truly pleases Him, and watch what happens with how things turn around for us when we heed His words in this way.

"They ask me to take action on their behalf,
pretending they want to be near me.
'We have fasted before you!' they say.
'Why aren't you impressed?
We have been very hard on ourselves,
and you don't even notice it!'

'I will tell you why!' I respond.
'It's because you are fasting to please yourselves.
Even while you fast,
you keep oppressing your workers.
What good is fasting
when you keep on fighting and quarreling?
This kind of fasting
will never get you anywhere with me.
You humble yourselves
by going through the motions of penance,
bowing your heads
like reeds bending in the wind.
You dress in burlap
and cover yourselves with ashes.
Is this what you call fasting?
Do you really think this will please the LORD?

No, this is the kind of fasting I want:
Free those who are wrongly imprisoned;
lighten the burden of those who work for you.
Let the oppressed go free,
and remove the chains that bind people.
Share your food with the hungry,
and give shelter to the homeless.
Give clothes to those who need them,
and do not hide from relatives who need your help.

Then your salvation will come like the dawn,
and your wounds will quickly heal.

> Your godliness will lead you forward,
> and the glory of the LORD will protect you from behind.
> Then when you call, the LORD will answer.
> 'Yes, I am here,' he will quickly reply.
>
> Remove the heavy yoke of oppression.
> Stop pointing your finger and spreading vicious rumors!
> Feed the hungry,
> and help those in trouble.
> Then your light will shine out from the darkness,
> and the darkness around you will be as bright as noon.
> The LORD will guide you continually,
> giving you water when you are dry
> and restoring your strength.
> You will be like a well-watered garden,
> like an ever-flowing spring." (Isaiah 58:2a-11 NLT)

It certainly cannot hurt, and surprisingly will only help and heal, if we merely step out and try the idea that loving God and loving others, in spite of our own pain, afflictions, pressures, grief—rather than waiting for it to go away first—would bring us to a place of freedom, peace, and healing due to a more solid, unshakable joy that isn't contingent on our current conditions at all. When our focus takes this life-changing shift of loving God and loving others, in spite of what we are personally going through, not only do we begin to breathe fresh air of more mental and emotional freedom, since we will naturally be helping ourselves get us and our pain off our minds easier; but we will also be able to enter the rest of God, trusting that He is actively at work on our own broken places of crisis and pain.

To lighten things up a bit, yet provide a valid example of when I decided to "step out and find out," as Joyce Meyer says, God had a sweet surprise for me one day, which might bring a smile to your face as it still does to mine. Hurricane Harvey had hit our area, which destroyed numerous homes; maybe even you personally relate, as many natural disasters have happened from East to West since then. This was a period in time when I was drowning emotionally by a hurricane of the soul, of which hardly anyone was aware since it was understandably overshadowed by the catastrophic storm. I was still reeling from the most painful, profound loss I had ever experienced of a family member with whom I was especially close. Physically, I was also in a bad place, with adrenal exhaustion and low thyroid that almost two years of medication trial and error still was not improving. Anyone who deals with this knows the spiral of depression, debilitating brain fog, and "whole body crashing" that naturally goes on with this type of condition. Furthermore, my job was falling apart; I was making a fraction of an income during the slowest season of the year. Even so, because I very thankfully had nowhere near the extent of property damage that others had experienced in the hurricane, I appeared "fine" as far as anyone knew from a distant acquaintance viewpoint. Only God was seeing my tears and personal struggles; but as I'm sure you're finding out, He is truly the only One Who matters and Who can help anyway!

As the nonprofit organization, Operation Blessing, came to provide disaster relief in our region, they needed hundreds of volunteers. My heart kept being so tugged about it, as a tender knocking of the Lord on the door of my heart, notwithstanding how broken it was and how fragile I felt. He was available to provide the strength if I would provide the "Yes, I will go." Despite my abounding weakness of anxieties galore, I signed up to go with a team to a home that was being rebuilt. I'll never forget the internal battle I had that one particular morning when all that was within me fought against it. This is the death to self I was talking about earlier for sure! Indeed, I was definitely being put to the test with this! In fact, as a testimony to how far God had brought me to this point, I had struggled in previous years with severe agoraphobia such that I could not leave home without debilitating panic attacks. Be encouraged, when you continue your journey with God without giving up, He will bring freedom in stages; and when He does, all sorts of hope opens to you. Had He not done such a liberating work in me over the years, this story never would have happened.

While working with the crew, a stray dog kept coming around our worksite. I loved him at first sight, as his eyes kept meeting mine. However, it was not safe or appreciated that he was around our work area. The person in charge kept trying to get rid of him, but he was quite persistent, as he was obviously starving, lost, and abandoned. The longer this went on, the more he became a nuisance to everyone, so I figured the best way I could help was to get him out of their way!

To make a long story short, God knows the very special inroad to my heart is my love for dogs. With all the courage and strength I had that day to help a family who had lost their home, little did I know God was going to surprise me with so much love and joy that very same day and beyond, which would help restore *my* home! Since I wasn't able to locate the dog's owner, this sweetest ever addition to the two other dogs I had—who had also been found roaming the streets—blended in so well, it was as if he had been with us forever. But the abundance of love I have received from this one dog especially, having nurtured him through the physical problems he had when I found him, has been a constant reminder of the point I'm making.

Had I wallowed in my own sorrow and suffering, closing my heart to the opportunity to help in the disaster relief of so many who had lost everything, I would have missed this incredible gift from God. It's a gift that has continued giving, so far beyond those days of my helping others. See how well God can multiply a harvest? To this day, as I hold this dog close and enjoy his cute personality with much laughter and special loving moments, I marvel at the healing balm this has had on my life—not only back then, but in an ongoing way.

Maybe you are not a dog lover, and if not, this story might not move you at all. That's okay! Whatever your love language is, I promise you, God knows how to speak it and reach you at your heart's door. I dare you to "step out and find out" by helping someone else in need. God will overcompensate you in blessings beyond your wildest dreams too! Every good and perfect gift comes from our Father, and with Him, there is no shadow of turning![5] Take a chance, be bold and courageous. Someone out there needs your help, and you will discover the richest, most abundant harvest and compensation of being helped and loved in extra special ways by God Himself every time!

In fact, speaking of how weak I felt in that situation, but encountered God's ability infused into me, brings me to the next point. There is no telling what God can and will do when we bring Him our weaknesses in exchange for His strength. No matter what lies behind the tears you cry, the powerlessness, vulnerability, anxiety, or pain you may be feeling, Jesus truly understands.

> "It was necessary for Him to be made in every respect like us, His brothers and sisters, so that He could be our merciful and faithful High Priest before God. Then He could offer a sacrifice that would take away the sins of the people. Since He Himself has gone through suffering and testing, He is able to help us when we are being tested" (Hebrews 2:17-18 NLT).

"So then, since we have a great High Priest Who has entered heaven, Jesus the Son of God, let us hold firmly to what we believe. This High Priest of ours understands our weaknesses, for He faced all of the same testings we do, yet He did not sin. So let us come boldly to the throne of our gracious God. There we will receive His mercy, and we will find grace to help when we need it most" (Hebrews 4:14-16 NLT). We can draw immeasurable comfort, strength, help, and hope in knowing Jesus is constantly praying for us: "He is able, once and forever, to save those who come to God through Him. He lives forever to intercede with God on their behalf" (Hebrews 7:25 NLT).

Paul must have surely grasped this reality as He experienced "more and more grace" for the weaknesses that he had called his "thorn in the flesh."[6] He prayed repeatedly that God would remove them, but instead, God's answer was no; He would rather make His strength perfect in those very weaknesses! How could we ask for anything more?

To have God's strength perfected where we are utterly weak, is actually better than having our weak areas removed altogether. Could it even be said that the weaker we are, the stronger God will show Himself to be? That is, our weaknesses make more room and prove greater need for Him to come in, fill us up, and make us strong. James 4:6 says that the ones who experience His grace the most are the ones lowly and humble enough to receive it. No wonder special needs children have such a dynamically clear view of God and seem so full of a peculiar light-hearted joy. Challenged as they are, it is not hard for them to realize their happiness comes from God loving them just as they are, completely separate from their own abilities or strengths. While they bring nothing to the table, God therefore brings it all; and behold, there is a feast of joy!

When we get broken down from a high place—prestige, success, great ability or achievement—and then we experience a fall—unemployment, accident, disaster, trauma, loss, illness—it can be a hard break indeed. Even so, it is for the broken that Jesus actually came. He has promised to be close to the brokenhearted and those who are crushed in spirit.[7] The greater our weaknesses, the deeper the capacity God has to make His strength known.

Tying this altogether in summary, a powerful motivator behind this entire process is ultimately to lead and encourage others to find Jesus, our only hope of a Savior, no matter how deep of a struggle in which we find ourselves. Although we may feel weak and therefore unable to carry on, it is in Jesus that we are actually made strong and indeed capable of finishing this race. Putting to death our old nature, including all our selfish desires or suicide exit strategies to escape the pain, we find our true worth of living in being solely alive unto God for His love to flow through us for the sake of others. It may not have been the death we thought we wanted; it's a death of an entirely different, self-less kind, but this is indeed the only way out of despair into hope.

"Whatever we do, it is certainly not for our own profit, but because Christ's love controls us now. Since we believe that Christ died for all of us, I should also believe that I have died to the old life I used to live.

He died for all so that all who live—having received eternal life from Him—might live no longer for themselves, to please themselves, but to spend their lives pleasing Christ Who died and rose again for them" (II Corinthians 5:14-15 TLB).

---

1 Romans 5:8

2 I Corinthians 6:20

3 Romans 6:6

4 II Corinthians 5:17

5 James 1:17

6 James 4:6 AMP, II Corinthians 12:8-10

7 Psalm 34:18

COMING OUT OF THE DARKNESS

Just as it has been scientifically proven that light has healing properties for those suffering from depression, since it raises serotonin levels; so is it true that light can bring healing to the heart and spirit. It is indeed fundamentally one of the first steps we can take in seeking hope. That is, when we allow God to shine the searchlights of heaven into our souls, exposing whatever darkness might be lurking there—past hurts, sins, roots of bitterness and resentment, seeds of deception, lust, addictions, and other hidden evils—we can find freedom and healing by coming into the light of His love, grace, and mercy. Psalm 27:1 says that God is our Light and our Salvation. From I John 1:5, we know that God is light, and in Him there is no darkness at all. Jesus said, "I am the light of the world. Anyone who follows me will never walk in darkness, but will have the light of life" (John 8:12 CSB).

Perhaps you are being abused and keeping the shame hidden in the darkness of your soul. Bringing this into the light by telling someone trustworthy is the first step towards finding freedom, healing, and hope. Even past abuse that has never been shared with anyone has a way of keeping us bound in the darkness of shame. While this is so hard to face, it is critical for deep, inner healing. Suicide is the not the way out, but the light of Jesus bringing healing to those painful wounds is, in fact, your better way out.

Since Satan is the prince of darkness, we are entertaining hell's powerful wrath and evil involvement of our lives when we withhold certain areas of our lives from the light. No wonder Jesus said that the truth will set us free (John 8:32), just like the darkness guarantees to keep us bound. Once the enemy has us hidden in the darkness of shame, depression easily settles in, and despair strangles us, choking all life from us if we let it. Although it may not feel like it when you are in such a dark pit, there really is light at the end of the tunnel. Obviously, it takes faith to believe this, but all you need is a small mustard seed size of faith. God can work with that; it was actually the illustration Jesus gave Himself since He knew we would find ourselves in situations where faith eluded us completely, with all hope apparently gone. Remember though, "Nothing is impossible for God" (Luke 1:37 CEV).

Are you contemplating suicide because you are in the grip of an addiction? I've been there. So have many other people I've heard through my involvement with Celebrate Recovery who went through hellacious experiences—serving time in prison, broken marriages, custody of children lost, estrangement from family, ruined health, mental breakdowns, and more—all as a result of how addictions ravage lives. You are not alone.

This is not a book written from a distance, such as a textbook of gathered research and scientific, psychological data. Not only is it grounded in personal experience, but also is based on the stories of others I personally know. Just recently, I heard a couple share their testimony. I had always respected and loved them as friends, and could tell that when they prayed for people, they carried a powerful God-given authority and anointing; but I never knew the extent of their background until they shared so openly and candidly where all they had been and how God has restored them from such dark places in life.

Both husband and wife had grown up in dysfunctional homes. The environments they grew up in had an absence of nurturing love, drug and alcohol addictions, instability, and volatility. As you can easily imagine, suicide temptation encroached upon my friend at a very young age. Thankfully, her attempt was not successful. Indeed, this story demonstrates what God can do when He intervenes and spares a precious life from the dark and deadly jaws of suicide.

Naturally, they grew up using drugs and alcohol themselves, even as children. In fact, the way they met each other was that one was the drug dealer for the other, while their relationship evolved into becoming parents of a surprise baby. Having almost overdosed on heroine, the mother tried to stop for the sake of her child, but indeed could not. Despite her time in jail and periods of homelessness, living in out-of-control brokenness, she eventually went to a rehab center that would take in both her three year old daughter and herself. Meanwhile, God was working on her other half, as he also finally surrendered to going into rehab at Teen Challenge. Huge chunks of brutally painful history filled these tender teenage years that involved much trauma, heartache, and untold miseries of bondage before they were finally willing to surrender and admit their need for help.

In other words, they both came out of darkness into the light, which began their journey to freedom. I also had to go to treatment centers. One size does not fit all, but I do know I've heard countless times how impossible it feels to conquer addictions all alone. It is a sign of strength, not weakness, to come out of the dark into the light, admitting your need for help and support. I promise, God will meet you there. Whereas God opposes the proud, He absolutely *loves* rising to the cry of helping the humble. Maybe this can encourage you to take a step in seeking such a place. Although their detox experiences differed drastically from each other, where one was considerably easier in a physical sense, God's grace abounded to both, and they broke free from those heavy chains that had bound them for so long.

Today, this couple stands so strong, healthy, and beautifully glowing. They now pray for others with a special anointing and strength because they have been through hell's worst and back, as it were, and now are unquestionably free. The daughter they had during their turbulent addiction years is truly a trophy of God's grace. Not only is she a gorgeous seventeen year old preparing to graduate from high school soon, but she is very gifted as a dancer. She has no physical or developmental problems, as one might have expected from the grim situation in which she was conceived. So she really is a beautiful miracle of how nothing is impossible for God. They also have another little girl—yet another testimony of God's reward of those who diligently seek Him. This young beauty is also a budding dancer with a grace that emanates God's fragrant presence and echoes His power from generation to generation. When I asked her one time if she practices a lot, she smiled and shook her head, "no." With humble simplicity, both girls just flow in the beauty and restoration of God's beautiful tapestry that has been woven into this family by His grace and powerful hand of salvation and redemption.

Again, although I had always loved them, I never knew their entire story before they shared it in full. Even this speaks volumes of how God brings beauty from ashes—not even leaving the smell of smoke or tainted marks of the enemy's destruction. Because of how strong they are—full of love, maturity in God, and healthy in every way, one could have never guessed the trauma and self-abuse they both suffered for so many years. This is what God could do when they were willing to come out of the darkness into His light of love, freedom, and truth. Remember, what He can do for one, He can do for another. Father God does not have any favorites![1]

Whatever source of shame is keeping you isolated in the darkness, convinced that you are beyond help and hope, understand that this is a famous lie of the enemy which is not true whatsoever. It may be shame of such magnitude that has buried you in self-hatred and hopelessness that the mere thought of seeking help is when you feel the most shame of all. This too, is just the familiar cycle that the enemy uses to keep you bound, which must be broken. Easier said than done? Of course it is! No one ever said this was easy, but there is life and freedom for you when you just take the first step. This is where you find the wealth of God's help just beginning.

The way bugs instantly scatter at the onset of light is the way our enemies will scatter when we come into the light of all God is—His love, truth, and presence.

> "May God arise, may His enemies be scattered; may His foes flee before Him. May you blow them away like smoke—as wax melts before the fire, may the wicked perish before God. But may the righteous be glad and rejoice before God; may they be happy and joyful. Sing to God, sing in praise of His name, extol Him Who rides on the clouds; rejoice before Him—His name is the Lord. A Father to the fatherless, a Defender of the widows, is God is His holy dwelling. God sets the lonely in families, He leads out the prisoners with singing; but the rebellious live in a sun-scorched land" (Psalm 68:1-6 NIV).

Although it may be painful, causing us to wince emotionally at the discomfort of having long-standing secrets or ways of life exposed in the revealing light of His countenance, it is for our good, just in the same way that we're glad to see the bugs go away when the light is turned on! His nature as our Light is to lead us out from our prison of despair, darkness, shame, and isolation, as He scatters our enemies. To be sure, Jesus says that the light always overcomes the darkness.[2] This can give us overwhelming hope, even when we find ourselves seemingly trapped and hemmed in on every side, in the darkest pit of despair.

I speak to you who are consumed by pornography, you who are involved in an adulterous affair, stealing and lying to cover your tracks, to you who have had an abortion and not only can't tell anyone, but cannot face yourself in the mirror, even feeling that you deserve to die yourself because of it. Each one of you who read this book with tear-stained face that there is no way out of your shame, there is a better way out than suicide. His name is Jesus. Listen closely to His Words:

"Say to the captives, 'Come out,' and to those in darkness, 'Be free!' …They will neither hunger nor thirst, nor will the desert heat or the sun beat upon them. He who has compassion on them will guide them and lead them beside springs of water… Shout for joy, O heavens; rejoice, O earth; burst into song, O mountains! For the Lord comforts His people and will have compassion on His afflicted ones.

But Zion said, 'The Lord has forsaken me, the Lord has forgotten me.' "Can a mother forget the baby at her breast and have no compassion on the child she has borne? Though she may forget, I will not forget you! See, I have engraved you on the palms of my hands; your walls are ever before me…

Then you will know that I am the Lord; those who hope in Me will not be disappointed…I will contend with those who contend with you, and your children I will save. I will make your oppressors eat their own flesh; they will be drunk on their own blood, as with wine. Then all mankind will know that I, the Lord, am your Savior, your Redeemer, the Mighty One of Jacob" (excerpts from Isaiah 49 NIV).

Are you able to hear the heart of the Lord Who is fervently fighting for you, because He holds your worth so high as to have you engraved on the palm of His hand? This is the God of your rescue. This is the One with Whom your breakthrough and breaking free begins. Notice how He starts calling—He says to come out of the darkness. It is your time to be free. The enemy lies to you that you don't deserve freedom or abundant life, but that is all it is, a lie. Have you ever been led on over time and lied to, but the liar was particularly good at the deception of it all that you didn't realize it until much later? Did you not feel duped and ever so foolish for not seeing it sooner? Well, you no longer have to play the fool. This is precisely what the enemy does; it's who he is—the father of lies. Wisdom whispers, and eventually shouts, for you to awaken and see it all for what it is.

Let the truth of Jesus set you free by taking that first step out of the darkness and shame to receive all that Jesus died to give you. God already expressed all His wrath on Jesus at the cross. Jesus was already punished in your place. There is no shame or condemnation from Him—only love, mercy, grace, and forgiveness—full of light and freedom. "Let the one who walks in the dark, who has no light, trust in the name of the Lord and rely on their God" (Isaiah 50:10b NIV). "He was pierced for our transgressions, He was crushed for our iniquities; the punishment that brought us peace was upon Him, and by His wounds we are healed" (Isaiah 53:5 NIV).

St. Augustine said, "Remember this. When people choose to withdraw from a fire, the fire continues to give warmth, but they grow cold. When people choose to withdraw far from the light, the light continues to be bright in itself, but they are in darkness. This is also the case when people withdraw from God."[3] So my prayer for you is that the eyes of your heart will be flooded with light so that you can know the hope to which you are called and the riches of His glorious inheritance that He has given you as one of His own.[4] To the same enemy who has had you playing the fool by lying to you, and you have believed him until now, this is what you are now able to say as you arise from your dark shadows and shame, "As for me, I watch in hope for the Lord, I wait for God my Savior; my God will hear me. Do not gloat over me, my enemy! Though I have fallen, I will rise. Though I sit in darkness, the Lord will be my light" (Micah 7:7-8 NIV).

> "You groped your way through that murk once, but no longer. You're out in the open now. The bright light of Christ makes your way plain. So no more stumbling around. Get on with it!
>
> The good, the right, the true—these are the actions appropriate for daylight hours. Figure out what will please Christ, and then do it. Don't waste your time on useless work, mere busywork, the barren pursuits of darkness. Expose these things for the sham they are. It's a scandal when people waste their lives on things they must do in the darkness where no one will see. Rip

the cover off those frauds and see how attractive they look in the light of Christ.

Wake up from your sleep,
Climb out of your coffins;
Christ will show you the light!

So watch your step. Use your head. Make the most of every chance you get. These are desperate times! Don't live carelessly, unthinkingly. Make sure you understand what the Master wants" (Ephesians 5:8-17 MSG).

Do you realize, you are actually chosen by God as a target of His love and presence? He cannot associate with darkness though, because He is Light! He has so much inheritance He wants to give you, but it requires coming into agreement with what He says about you, and coming into the light of His love to receive it! "You are a chosen people, a royal priesthood, a holy nation, God's special possession, that you may declare the praises of Him Who called you out of darkness into His wonderful light" (I Peter 2:9 NIV).

Remember, nothing in this entire book has a trace of condemnation in it. We have all sinned and fallen short of God's glory.[5] So if secret sins and shame are what have you bound in the darkness, all you need to do is come to Jesus with a broken, contrite heart. That is what He promises never to refuse. Receiving His forgiveness is like being without electricity for a long time, groping in the darkness, unable to find your way, frustrated and miserable that nothing is working; when suddenly, the lights come back on and waves of relief wash all over you that you can get back to living again. Hear it in a new way:

"This is the message we have heard from Him and declare to you: God is light; in Him there is no darkness at all. If we claim to have fellowship with Him yet walk in the darkness, we lie and do not live out the truth. But if we walk in the light, as He is in the light, we have fellowship with one another, and the blood of Jesus, His Son, purifies us from all sin. If we claim to be without sin, we deceive ourselves and the truth is not in us. If we confess our sins, He is faithful and just and will forgive us our sins and purify us from all unrighteousness" (I John 1:5-9 NIV).

Receive with great joy and relief the invitation from Jesus to come out of the darkness into His light and love. He truly is singing over you, interceding for you, and fighting your battles for you more than you are consciously aware. In fact, He wins every time! This is how the Psalmist David celebrated such a reality.

> "You, O Lord, keep my lamp burning;
> my God turns my darkness into light.
> With Your help, I can advance against a troop;
> with my God I can scale a wall.
> As for God, His way is perfect; the word of the Lord is flawless.
> He shields all who take refuge in Him.
> For who is God besides the Lord?
> And who is the Rock except our God?
> It is God who arms me with strength and keeps my way secure.
> He makes my feet like the feet of a deer;
> He enables me to stand on the heights.
> He trains my hands for battle;
> my arms can bend a bow of bronze.
> You make Your saving help my shield,
> and Your right hand sustains me;
> Your help has made me great.
> You provide a broad path for my feet,
> so that my ankles do not give way.
> I pursued my enemies and overtook them;
> I did not turn back till they were destroyed.
> I crushed them so that they could not rise; they fell beneath my feet.
> You armed me with strength for the battle;
> You humbled my adversaries before me.
> You made my enemies turn their backs in flight,
> and I destroyed my foes…
> The Lord lives! Praise be to my Rock! Exalted be God my Savior!

He is the God Who avenges me…"
(Psalm 18:28-47a NIV)

To end this chapter, hear the call to come out of the darkness straight from God's own words of what His heart is for us when we are groping in the dark, unable to find our way. Are you afraid to come out of the darkness into the light? Is the bright light actually painful to your eyes while you are in this pit of depression? Are you frightened by your own vulnerabilities once you come into the bright light? God is already there, making a way for you to be safe. Jesus completely understands where you are. He is bringing justice to your situation where you have been treated unfairly. His heart beats for the hurting ones in the dark shadows. Listen to what He says He will do for you in helping you escape the prison of darkness and embrace the truth by living in the light.

> "'Take a good look at my servant.
> I'm backing him to the hilt.
> He's the one I chose,
> and I couldn't be more pleased with him.
> I've bathed him with my Spirit, my *life*.
> He'll set everything right among the nations.
> He won't call attention to what he does
> with loud speeches or gaudy parades.
> He won't brush aside the bruised and the hurt
> and he won't disregard the small and insignificant,
> but he'll steadily and firmly set things right.
> He won't tire out and quit. He won't be stopped
> until he's finished his work—to set things right on earth.
> Far-flung ocean islands
> wait expectantly for his teaching.'
> GOD's Message,
> the God who created the cosmos, stretched out the skies,
> laid out the earth and all that grows from it,
> Who breathes life into earth's people,

makes them alive with his own life:
'I am GOD. I have called you to live right and well.
I have taken responsibility for you, kept you safe.
I have set you among my people to bind them to me,
and provided you as a lighthouse to the nations,
To make a start at bringing people into the open, into light:
opening blind eyes,
releasing prisoners from dungeons,
emptying the dark prisons.
I am GOD. That's my name.
I don't franchise my glory,
don't endorse the no-god idols.
Take note: The earlier predictions of judgment have been fulfilled.
I'm announcing the new salvation work.
Before it bursts on the scene,
I'm telling you all about it.'
Sing to GOD a brand-new song,
sing his praises all over the world!
Let the sea and its fish give a round of applause,
with all the far-flung islands joining in.
Let the desert and its camps raise a tune,
calling the Kedar nomads to join in.
Let the villagers in Selah round up a choir
and perform from the tops of the mountains.
Make GOD's glory resound;
echo his praises from coast to coast.
GOD steps out like he means business.
You can see he's primed for action.
He shouts, announcing his arrival;
he takes charge and his enemies fall into line:
'I've been quiet long enough.
I've held back, biting my tongue.
But now I'm letting loose, letting go,
like a woman who's having a baby—Stripping the hills bare,
withering the wildflowers,

> Drying up the rivers,
> turning lakes into mudflats.
> But I'll take the hand of those who don't know the way,
> who can't see where they're going.
> I'll be a personal guide to them,
> directing them through unknown country.
> I'll be right there to show them what roads to take,
> make sure they don't fall into the ditch.
> These are the things I'll be doing for them—
> sticking with them, not leaving them for a minute.'"
> (Isaiah 42:1-16 MSG)

---

1 Shared with permission, names withheld; Acts 10:34

2 John 1:5

3 Saint Augustine, "When People Withdraw." (Updated January 21, 2017). *The Catholic Storeroom*. http://www.catholicstoreroom.com/2017/01/21/when-people-withdraw/ (Accessed December 29, 2020).

4 Ephesians 1:18

5 Romans 3:23

IN GOD WE TRUST—OR NOT

Our coins in America claim that we trust in God, but do we really? It sounds good, and we casually assume that we do trust God, but do we in the deepest, personal, individual way truly trust Him? It is true that actions speak louder than words. So even though it makes a good-sounding phrase that we trust God, many times our struggles with anxiety, depression, discontentment, and often fearful mindsets suggest otherwise, especially when so far as to contemplate suicide.

As you have noticed by now, I have to lighten things up a bit occasionally to draw pictures with words. God does this with me, so it tends to be my style of communicating. A unique way of showing me the truth in my own heart, God has used my dogs to show me how loving, or hurtful, our trust in Him (or lack thereof) can be. Even if you are not an animal lover, perhaps you can still appreciate the lesson behind this word picture of a parallel.

Two dogs I had years ago struggled with separation anxiety for seemingly different reasons. Each in their own right paints a different color to this truth-filled lesson of the heart. When my Golden Retriever passed away at age sixteen, not only did my own heart break, as she was an incredible dog whom I loved dearly; but this left her best friend, my smaller dog then age thirteen, feeling so forlorn and forsaken. They had grown up together and were truly inseparable. Since the younger one had never been alone a single day of her life, she suffered from grief and depression in the most profound way, not the least of which was a terrible case of separation anxiety. Obviously, my love for her had not changed in the slightest way whatsoever; in fact, I certainly shared her pain and felt tremendous compassion for her in the painful stages of grief. However, as I observed her even withdrawing at my loving attempts to comfort her—in every *other* way besides being able to bring her big friend back—her behavior demonstrated anxiety so severe that she might as well have been telling me, "I don't trust you anymore." Even after all thirteen years of her life, in which I had poured vast amounts of love, time, care, and all sparing no expense, she began doubting my love or care *now*? She would look at me with those eyes widened with fright and unbelief, a wavering trust indeed, every time I attempted to leave, for example. Because I knew I had done absolutely everything within my power to make her peaceful and comfortable, happy and content, it truly broke my heart that she seemed to stop trusting me as a result of her grieving—either that I would not return, or that she wouldn't be fed her next meal, or whatever the "fear" within her mind was—although her whole life she was never left without my returning, or missed a meal!

Another rescue dog I had drives home the same truth from another angle. She came to me as the one nobody wanted. Having been abandoned, rejected, and was facing euthanasia at the city's high kill pound, she found a home not only in my house, but in my heart. Surprisingly, however, she presented herself to be the most ungrateful, picky eater I had ever seen in canines *or* humans! I could certainly understand that with so much unknown baggage of possible abuse, she would have had major issues with trust. It even makes perfect sense that separation anxiety would have evoked her fears and triggered her past traumas in a most powerful way. However, it simply took me by such surprise that she did not seem to have the slightest bit of gratitude for food, no matter how much painstaking effort, time, and expense I invested in trying to make it as pleasingly palatable as possible. I knew it wasn't an appetite problem, as she danced around me in the kitchen with excitement during the preparation, wanting to lick my hands with all the eagerness as if to say, "Oh please hurry, I'm so hungry!" But then, a spitting it out type of picking once she had the bowl in front of her implied she didn't fully trust that I was giving her such wholesome nutrition after all. In fact, she looked up at me as if to question, "Really?" It was extremely odd, especially after so many years when some of my greatest pleasures have been to see my other dogs through the years gratefully and joyfully devour the food I prepared for them with such ecstatic zeal that I found myself even looking forward to getting to feed them again; because I just adored their grateful trust and reliance in my ability to provide something they could enjoy so much.

In fact, I piercingly recall when my Golden had her stroke, and those excruciating few days that followed, in which we were trying so hard to say goodbye to each other. What I keenly remember as one of the most tender moments of all is how she put forth extreme efforts to eat what I had prepared for her, even though she could not even lift or hold up her own head. She had grown in my love and trust so much that she knew I was giving her the absolute best possible nutrition; and not only did she enjoy the taste in a grateful, exuberant way (yes, even in spite of a stroke!), but more importantly, she loved—as I did—the nurturing we shared as she zealously devoured my loving creation. She never vacillated in trust of me, just as she never wavered in knowing how much she was loved. Hence, she never struggled one day with separation anxiety, although she actually was my only dog at the very beginning, and was left alone for a full day's work without a single problem. In other words, the one having every reason to struggle simply didn't, all because she knew deeply in a fixed, internal, wholeheartedly trusting way that I "would never leave her or forsake her" (as God tells us), and I would always take utmost delight in meeting her every need, including bringing her life as much joy and fun as possible!

As I've pondered these canine parallels of how my own heart trusts God, or not, I realized that much of my anxiety has been admittedly based on the faulty notion that God might not come through like I am so hoping or expecting Him to do. Now you see why I provided those examples of what I must have looked like in a human way! Sometimes, God needs to drop a veil over our emotions that may blanket His presence from being as bright or close as we desire it to be, all so that we can learn to grow in deeper trust of Him, instead of relying on emotional highs as if to equate happiness with His presence. While He created us to have, creatively use, and enjoy our emotions as part of what makes us whole, He doesn't want us to rely solely on what we feel as a way of experiencing relationship with Him. He desires for us so much more than that. It is trust that He longs to establish deep within our hearts, so that we can remain unshaken and stable even when hard times occur and seem to rock our very foundation. When we truly trust Him with our lives, we will have an ability to stay solid and secure in His love, to the point that the world around us may not understand; and therefore, provide us the opportunity to glorify Him *through* the fires of difficulty, even if and when not immediately delivered *from* them.

When God seemingly withdraws His presence—at least insofar as our emotions perceive—He is actually as close as He always was, and always will be; because this is His promise from His own Word, which will never return void. It is as a cloudy sky. Just because we cannot see the sun shining when the clouds are so dense and dark just before a heavy rainfall, does not mean the sun is not shining bright on the other side. In Jeremiah 33:25-26, He says that breaking His covenant with His children would be like breaking covenant with day and night, or all of nature; and He simply cannot and will never do this! He says that just in the same way as nature keeps working according to covenant plan of night and day, earth and sky, so will He continue in covenantal relationship with us as a Father to His children, never to reject and abandon us! Remember, He is not like earthly fathers, which can fail, disappoint, reject, abuse, or abandon their children due to their own brokenness. God is always worthy of our trust, because He absolutely *never* fails. He literally cannot lie or prove false. His Word endures forever.

If we trust in our finances, we are trusting in something that has failure-potential. Thus, our trust runs the risk of being shaken when the economy takes a turbulent turn. If we trust in other people, or even in our companion animals, for the love we seek, we face impending hurt, loss, and other disappointments and failures. It all depends where our trust truly is placed that will determine how stable our lives are. God is the only stability we will ever find in this life. He is utterly trustworthy to take care of us and meet our every need, which He has promised to do through Jesus. "This same God who takes care of me will supply all your needs from His glorious riches, which have been given to us in Christ Jesus" (Philippians 4:19 NLT).

To further the parallel with my dogs, I find that the absolute best way they can show me genuine love is to trust me; and conversely, the most hurtful way they can insult me is not to trust me. This surely reflects how it must be with our relationship to God. We are loving Him most when we are trusting Him wholeheartedly—holding nothing back—not our secret reservations and doubts that "just in case He doesn't come through, I've got this to fall back on." Or, "I'll try to pray, but if He doesn't come through by Wednesday, I'm going to end it all; I just can't take this anymore."

Psalm 89:8 TLB says, "Faithfulness is Your very character." If you have not walked with God long enough to know this personally, that's okay. Build your faith from others who have lived in history—in the Bible, such as in Hebrews 11, or survivors like Corrie Ten Boom who endured such harsh treatment in the Ravensbruck concentration camp during World War II—whose faith emerged all the stronger having journeyed through the rugged terrain of tests and trials.[1] In Romans 4:18-25, Abraham believed God, even though all human reason for hope was gone; and this was credited to him as righteousness. God does not overlook our faith; it is no doubt one of the most loving acts of worship we can give, especially when it seems like, as it did in

Abraham's case, that our believing in God at such a time, or in such a circumstance, is completely ridiculous. God had promised him that he would be the father of many nations, yet many years passed before he saw this fulfilled. At the time of being given the promise, he was very old, impotent, and his wife also in her nineties, well past a child-bearing age! Can you imagine what kind of faith and trust it took for Abraham to believe God at His Word? From God's perspective, it is our way of loving Him when we trust Him through the darkest, hardest times when all seems bleak and hopeless to our natural eyes. He actually promises to reward those who diligently seek Him.[2]

Just because it may seem that God has distanced Himself from you in your darkest hour, please know it is not the case at all. Remember the cloudy sky at such a time. The sun (like the Son of God) is still shining just as brightly as always; there is just a veil (of clouds, or difficulty) shielding our vision from seeing or feeling Him as clearly as we wish we could. It doesn't mean He isn't still there, because He certainly is. When a shadow is cast over our emotional perception of His glory and presence, which makes it seem harder to hear, see, or experience Him on an emotional level, a way to honor Him would be to trust Him perhaps even all the more. Predictably, our faith will come forth tested and tried as pure gold refined in the fire. This is God's goal for us all—that we grow strong in our roots of faith in Him, so that nothing whatsoever can move us, shake us into panic, anxiety, or despair, or threaten our relationship with Him. After all, He promises us that *nothing* can ever separate us from His love.[3]

When Corrie Ten Boom was released from Ravensbruck, her faith had grown all the stronger and deeper as her love for Jesus, and His love for her, had seen her through her darkest hours, certainly her "valley of the shadow of death" (Psalm 23:4). This is how God wants it to be for us too. He longs to be our trusted Shepherd through the valley of the shadow of death, so that when we reach the other side of victory, we will have a stronger, experientially tested and tried kind of faith and love for Him that will enrich our character for His glory.

Think of the Olympics. My favorite part is watching them run with the torch! If we can think of Christianity as a way of passing on the burning torch, it will encourage us never to give up too soon; but rather, to keep trusting, even when we cannot see the finish line yet. Suicide temptation lures us into a quick finish, but the result is cheap grace and trashed faith. We lose, and we forfeit our opportunity to pass the baton, as it were, to the next runner in line after us. This is exactly what the enemy wants. He tempts us to give up, to stop believing, to think that our lives don't matter in the greater scheme of things; but all these are lies, coming straight from the father of lies—the devil. Our lives are indeed integral place markers, baton passers, milestone makers, and future trophies of grace in this great race of faith; but we must press forward to win the prize!

Let me end this chapter by sharing the full story of what Abraham's faith actually looked like. You will easily see why God used such a dramatic hopeless condition as his to speak, and later fulfill, such a promise. It was all to demonstrate to us what trusting God can do, even when it requires believing Him against all odds and when all hope seems lost.

> "So how do we fit what we know of Abraham, our first father in the faith, into this new way of looking at things? If Abraham, by what he *did* for God, got God to approve him, he could certainly have taken credit for it. But the story we're given is a God-story, not an Abraham-story. What we read in Scripture is, 'Abraham entered into what God was doing for him, and *that* was the turning point. He trusted God to set him right instead of trying to be right on his own.'
>
> If you're a hard worker and do a good job, you deserve your pay; we don't call your wages a gift. But if you see that the job is too big for you, that it's something only God can do, and you trust him to do it—you could never do it for yourself no matter how hard and long you worked—well, that trusting-him-to-do-it is what gets you set right with God, *by* God. Sheer gift.

David confirms this way of looking at it, saying that the one who trusts God to do the putting-everything-right without insisting on having a say in it is one fortunate man:

Fortunate those whose crimes are carted off,
whose sins are wiped clean from the slate.
Fortunate the person against whom the Lord does not keep score.

Do you think for a minute that this blessing is only pronounced over those of us who keep our religious ways and are circumcised? Or do you think it possible that the blessing could be given to those who never even heard of our ways, who were never brought up in the disciplines of God? We all agree, don't we, that it was by embracing what God did for him that Abraham was declared fit before God?

Now *think*: Was that declaration made before or after he was marked by the covenant rite of circumcision? That's right, before he was marked. That means that he underwent circumcision as evidence and confirmation of what God had done long before to bring him into this acceptable standing with himself, an act of God he had embraced with his whole life.

And it means further that Abraham is father of *all* people who embrace what God does for them while they are still on the "outs" with God, as yet unidentified as God's, in an "uncircumcised" condition. It is precisely these people in this condition who are called "set right by God and with God"!

Abraham is also, of course, father of those who have undergone the religious rite of circumcision not just because of the ritual but because they were willing to live in the risky faith-embrace of God's action for them, the way Abraham lived long before he was marked by circumcision.

That famous promise God gave Abraham—that he and his children would possess the earth—was not given because of something Abraham did or would do. It was based on God's decision to put everything together for him, which Abraham then entered when he believed. If those who get what God gives them only get it by doing everything they are told to do and filling out all the right forms properly signed, that eliminates personal trust completely and turns the promise into an ironclad *contract*! That's not a holy promise; that's a business deal. A contract drawn up by a hard-nosed lawyer and with plenty of fine print only makes sure that you will never be able to collect. But if there is no contract in the first place, simply a *promise*—and God's promise at that—you can't break it.

This is why the fulfillment of God's promise depends entirely on trusting God and his way, and then simply embracing him and what he does. God's promise arrives as pure gift. That's the only way everyone can be sure to get in on it, those who keep the religious traditions *and* those who have never heard of them. For Abraham is father of us all. He is not our racial father—that's reading the story backward. He is our *faith* father.

We call Abraham "father" not because he got God's attention by living like a saint, but because God made something out of Abraham when he was a nobody. Isn't that what we've always read in Scripture, God saying to Abraham, "I set you up as father of many peoples"?

Abraham was first named "father" and then *became* a father because he dared to trust God to do what only God could do: raise the dead to life, with a word make something out of nothing. When everything was hopeless, Abraham believed anyway, deciding to live not on the basis of what he saw he *couldn't* do but on what God said he *would* do. And so he was made father of a multitude of peoples. God himself said to him, 'You're going to have a big family, Abraham!'

Abraham didn't focus on his own impotence and say, 'It's hopeless. This hundred-year-old body could never father a child.' Nor did he survey Sarah's decades of infertility and give up. He didn't tiptoe around God's promise asking cautiously skeptical questions.

He plunged into the promise and came up strong, ready for God, sure that God would make good on what he had said. That's why it is said, 'Abraham was declared fit before God by trusting God to set him right.'

But it's not just Abraham; it's also us! The same thing gets said about us when we embrace and believe the One who brought Jesus to life when the conditions were equally hopeless. The sacrificed Jesus made us fit for God, set us *right with God*" (Romans 4 MSG).

---

1 Ten Boom, Corrie; Sherrill, John and Elizabeth. *The Hiding Place*. (Uhrichsville, OH: Barbour and Company, Inc., 1971).

2 Hebrews 11:6

3 Romans 8:38-39

HIS WOUNDS HAVE PAID OUR RANSOM

Are you intent on punishing yourself for something you have done, or perhaps for the shame of something done to you? In this context, you may be tempted to think that suicide is the answer. Guilt and shame can prove to be a such a perilous, painful bondage. Because of Jesus' finished work on the cross, however, it is unnecessary. He has destined you for more.

As previously shared, my hardest struggle of all was self-punishment, not simply being "hard on myself," but a lifestyle of self-abusive behavior as a form of penance for the guilt and shame that was forever weighing heavily upon me. Although it took years of relearning and retraining my brain to think new ways, to embrace my forgiven state, and to receive the gift of redemption and freedom that the Blood of Jesus made possible, such wonderful healing began taking root in my mind, replacing all those deeply established ruts and addictive patterns. Because a self-punitive way of survival was my ingrained way of life for so long, it took considerable time, faith, and effort to learn what true "living" really was instead of merely existing in an identity of shame. Reading, learning, and internalizing the Word helped me understand my true identity in Christ. This so liberated me, and the same can happen for you.

Do you relate to the self-degrading, self-mutilating, and self-punishing lifestyle? The temptation of suicide commonly follows when we travel this way for so long. How I would love to short circuit your pain and torment by sharing a few things that helped me break free. Give the truth a chance. Suicide is not your only way out. An altogether new identity is readily available for you that is so far removed from guilt and shame. Jesus wants to clothe you with a robe of righteousness. He personally took your shame, so He could give you His righteousness (right standing with God) in exchange.

It actually insults Jesus when we attempt to punish ourselves for the guilt and shame we feel. He paid such a high price of shedding His own royal, holy Blood so that we would not have to incur God's wrath or pay the debts we owed; nor would we have to live under a heavy identity of shame anymore. If you will simply come to Him, admitting how broken you are with all the failure, pain, and shame you might feel, you will be surprised and amazed at how His love and redemption will break through for you. He's just waiting on those walls to come down and allowing Him entrance into your heart, because He never forces Himself on us. He really has made atonement for us already; we only need to receive His finished work, and enter into His rest.

Do you know what His last words were when He was dying for you? "It is finished!" What did He mean by this? He was referring to the completion of what the Father had asked of Him—taking upon Himself all the sins of everyone, including their fullest penalties and punishments—bearing the entire dark weight of it all, so that we could live as free people, never needing to encounter God's wrath ever again. Yes, this is what Jesus finished for us! Entering into His rest simply means that we no longer doubt or waver; we absolutely believe Him at His Word that what He has said, accomplished, and promised is true.

After all, shame is a mean beast, and because it's the enemy's territory, he brings other evils with it, such as fear and doubt, bitterness and hatred. So even if it's only directed toward ourselves, we may be imprisoned by unforgiveness or bitterness. When we don't forgive ourselves or others, it is like drinking poison, while hoping the other person dies. Are you bitter against yourself, hoping you will die, because you hate yourself so much? Is this why your suicide temptation is so strong? This may understandably be the underlying root of bondage, decay, and despair. However, it's exactly the doom that the enemy would have you believe, which is completely unnecessary and false!

Again, what Jesus said was finished, by His extensive sacrificial death, has made a way for you to end this brutal war you have with yourself. You don't have to hold such bitterness against your life anymore. No matter what you've done, even if it has involved taking an innocent life such as in abortion, Jesus has already paid the price for your punishment. You can be absolutely and completely forgiven. He promises that He casts our sins from us as far as the east is from the west. Be encouraged as you read Psalm 103 to see how He treats us in spite of our sins. Besides removing them from us as far as the east is from the west, He does not chide or hold His anger forever. Do you know that this was even true before Jesus died for us? Yes, it really gives us a great picture of God's character, because this was how He treated His wayward children from the beginning of time. He does not hold a grudge, pure and simple.

Because He is holy, however, He has always required a sacrifice to be made for sin. This is why you find the Old Testament full of all that was necessary—the sacrificing of animals to make atonement for the sins of the people. A scapegoat took away their sins, yet this practice had to be done repeatedly, which proves the amazement of what Jesus later did in "finishing the work" of making His own Sacrifice the final end to all that. When Jesus died, He became our scapegoat. This officially ended the requirement for there to be any sacrifices made in terms of killing animals on an altar, like it was under the Old Covenant. What this means for us is that there leaves no room for questioning or doubting if we can truly live in a forgiven, freed state. Jesus accomplished (finished and paid in full) the payments of all we owed, due to our sins and failures. We can accept and appropriate His finished work on the Cross and never look back over our shoulder to our past mistakes. It is over forever! We do not have to keep punishing ourselves!

Follow me back in time to 2002 for a personal story that changed my life, which inspired this specific chapter. I began to get a revelation of this sacrifice that Jesus made "once and for all" by reading the book of Hebrews. I'm an avid reader, so typically, I read at least one or more books per week. However, that particular year, I was so captivated by the book of Hebrews that no other book could hold my attention. The insatiable hunger I had kept stirring me for more. Every chance I had for reading, I found myself turning to Hebrews; I truly could not get enough! This lasted an entire year. To this day, I cannot read it without being moved to tears and remembering that pivotal year, when all the darkness of my life and painful ways gave way to the light and truth of His Word setting me free. Have you ever been so engrossed in a subject that your fascination only grew the more you explored into it? Well, this happened to me with that special book in the Bible. I hungered so deeply that I wanted to delve into it in different versions of the Bible, just to hear it afresh and grasp it for all it's worth. All the cross references that various versions have, I traced as if searching for gold. It sent me to Leviticus a lot, where I learned all about the sacrifices the people in the Old Testament had to do. I saw striking parallels with my own life with that, because in essence, all my self-punishment was quite the same! My self-punishing behaviors were a vicious, repetitive cycle because they were never enough; the guilt and shame never lifted. The priests that offered the sacrifices for the people literally had to "keep standing," symbolizing that the process would need to be repeated; it was never completely sufficient to take away sin. This is why it was so significant that when Jesus as our High Priest accomplished the ultimate Sacrifice of offering Himself for our atonement of sins, He "sat down" at God's right hand, as the enemy was made a footstool for His feet (Hebrews 10:11-14). It meant that what He finished was final and lasting for all time, and for all of us. Isn't that powerful?

This is one of many examples of precisely how and when the Word becoming flesh (which is Jesus) changed my entire way of thinking and living. I dare you to read the book of Hebrews! Start with a version easy to understand and go from there. See how God speaks to you in showing you the reality of what Jesus paid, "once and for all" so that you and I no longer have to atone for our sins anymore. He truly paid our ransom when He was wounded on the Cross. That means we go free! Our freedom literally cost Jesus His very life. It was by no means "free"; it cost Him absolutely everything. Yet He did it for the sheer love of you. He wants you, He died for you. What longing He has for you to receive your freedom from Him as a gift!

Take the challenge to forgive yourself (and anyone else who has hurt or offended you). Forgiveness really does set us free in so many ways. First of all, you will notice the torment that you've been experiencing will dissipate. You will no longer be enslaved to that bondage of seeking vengeance gripping you. Have you realized how much mental energy you've been expending in all the thoughts of how you want that person to pay for what they have done, even if that person is yourself? Maybe you are keeping yourself or someone else hostage to your intentions of getting revenge. For so many years, I lived in this trap. I lived in a vicious cycle of self-punishment such that I made myself pay for my wrongs, and even took it out on myself when I was hurt by others. In other words, I made my own body the target of the wrath I felt, either towards myself or towards others. This seemed safe, as it certainly was no earthly crime to self-destruct. Yet, in God's eyes, it was definitely a criminal offense. He puts it this way, "Do you not know that your body is a temple of the Holy Spirit who is within you, whom you have [received as a gift] from God, and that you are not your own [property]? You were bought with a price [you were actually purchased with the precious blood of Jesus and made His own]. So then, honor and glorify God with your body" (I Corinthians 6:19-20 AMP).

Seeking vengeance toward ourselves or others is to remain in the bondage of unforgiveness, which is all so unnecessary. You will notice over time what a tremendous toll it takes on you physically, emotionally, and mentally, not to mention the corrosion of your spirit and soul, like rust that eventually renders moving parts utterly stuck and unusable. It is like putting a bird in a cage outside. Although it sees the freedom of the blue sky and all the trees and seeds it could be enjoying, it remains caged and bound to artificial branches. Nothing living is in the cage, which causes the bird to pine away, naturally yearning for all the life teeming beyond the cage door's lock. This bird is you, or me, when we choose to make ourselves or someone else pay for the painful hurt or offense we have committed or experienced. Only when we forgive completely, and no longer require payment or seek vengeance, the cage door is opened and the bird can fly freely again.

This is the freedom we all obviously want. Nothing compares to the lightness one feels after making the hard choice to forgive ourselves or someone else. It really is the most freeing experience in the world! Jesus truly did pay it all! Suicide is not your only way out of this misery. Forgiveness will unlock your emotional and mental prison, as it sets you free to live and not die. Remember, what Jesus accomplished was the penalty paid in full—once and for all—without our adding anything to it. When we trust His sacrificial gift of atonement instead of punishing, abusing, destroying, or killing ourselves, we show loyalty and love to Him, which then evokes His favor and blessing upon our lives. That is, through His cleansing Blood shed on the cross, He will remove the curse of bitterness and sin in our sweet surrender, forgiveness of others (including ourselves), and genuine repentance. Consequently, a new life opens in a hope-filled way to us in exchange for that heavily oppressive, despairing death grip.

I challenge you to come to Him broken and wounded, simply to receive His gift of love and forgiveness that poured out holy Blood at the Cross and still speaks a better word today than vengeance. "You have come to Jesus, the One Who mediates the new covenant between

God and people, and to the sprinkled blood, which speaks of forgiveness instead of crying out for vengeance…" (Hebrews 12:24 NLT). His wounds truly have paid your ransom. No more condemnation. No more punishing yourself by way of slow and subtle or deliberate suicide. No more despair and imprisonment from the depression of it all. You can go free even today! Jesus paid it all in full for you.

EVERY LIFE MATTERS

Each and every life God made is considered deeply precious to Him. It is not about how worthless you may feel. God has an entirely different perspective as our Creator. According to Psalm 139, we were delicately knit together in our mothers' wombs; and our days were planned in detail by God before even one of them took shape! Only God saw our unformed substances; but even then, He declared us beautiful in His eyes and worth the death of His own Son to have us be forever His.

When we take into account the Price that was paid for our ransom from an eternal death and separation from God, it gives us a taste into the kind of unconditional love God has for us. In other words, He brought you into the world knowing ahead of time the sins you would commit, the temptations you would have, including the fact that you would reach a point of not wanting to live anymore. It cost Him the greatest Sacrifice that was ever made in all of history; yet because of His everlasting love for us, He considered us worth it. For those tempted with suicide, the enemy's counterfeit lie has been a sense of worthlessness that he puts on us. Don't be deceived by him anymore. You are of infinite value to God, which He proved by sending Jesus to bleed to death for you, that you would be rescued from that stronghold of worthlessness.

Romans 5:8 NASB says, "God demonstrates His own love toward us, in that while we were still sinners, Christ died for us." It is one thing for a man to die for someone who is good and noble; but it is quite another dramatic picture that One would die for someone who is wretched and altogether evil, which is what we all are apart from Jesus. There is nothing whatsoever that you could do, or have already done, to nullify your worth in God's eyes or cause Him to stop loving you. Remember, love is a covenant word, not to mention the very definition of Who God is (I John 4:8).

> "This is what the LORD, your Creator says,...
> And He who formed you,...
> Do not fear, for I have redeemed you [from captivity];
> I have called you by name; you are Mine!
>
> When you pass through the waters, I will be with you;
> And through the rivers, they will not overwhelm you.
> When you walk through fire, you will not be scorched,
> Nor will the flame burn you.
>
> For I am the LORD your God,
> The Holy One of Israel, your Savior;...
>
> Because you are precious in My sight,
> You are honored and I love you,
> I will give *other* men in return for you
> and *other* peoples in exchange for your life.
> Do not fear, for I am with you..."
> (ISAIAH 43:1-5a AMP)

You may have grown up believing that you were a mistake—perhaps the result of an unplanned pregnancy or otherwise an unwanted surprise. In Psalm 51:5, David says that sin was even present at the time he was brought forth from his mother's womb. We do live in such a broken world that even events which seem like they should possess such a pure, innocent quality as conception and childbirth still come under the evil sway of our day, subject to the fallen nature of humanity. This, however, does not diminish our lives as touched by the Divine. Job 33:4 says that it is the Spirit of God that made us, and the breath of the Almighty that gives us life. "The decision is wholly of the Lord, even the events that seem accidental are really ordered by Him" (Proverbs 16:33 AMPC).

Rejection may permeate your entire life story, with early beginnings and an end of it not even felt yet, if it is an ongoing present painful happening even now for you. However, through this piercing pain, God is actually giving us a privilege in this golden opportunity to share in the sufferings of Christ, so that we may later share in His glory.[1] Jesus suffered such unjust rejection Himself. After all, He was literally God in fleshly form, yet despised by many. Not only so, but He came to earth to be among His own people; yet even they did not welcome Him, believe Him to be Who He said He was, or accept Him as being true. Can you imagine how much this must have hurt Him? To this day, many Jews—those whom He loves so very much—still reject Him to this day. It amazes me how His love burns strongly unchanging, from past history to present days, in spite of this.

What captures my attention even more is that He kept *us* in mind as His *joy* that He literally endured the cross with love for us in mind.[2] That is, He put all that rejection and shame in carrying our sins out of His focus while He was being abused and tortured on the Cross; because He knew the reconciliation He was making possible in those dark, painful hours would be so worth it. He kept His gaze forward on this, while ignoring the shame and pain of rejection He had experienced. We were considered worth it to Him to have suffered so intensely.

Surely we can rise to follow His example, in spite of all we have experienced, or maybe are still currently enduring. Like Peter said, it's not necessarily noteworthy if someone suffers for doing wrong; but it's when the suffering is unjust and undeserved, we can have the hope of sharing in Christ's glory as a result of remaining true to Him no matter what.[3]

Of course, when we're so low that we're tempted with suicide, convinced that our lives don't even matter anyway, it's especially hard to keep our eyes focused on the future. We simply want out of our intense pain "now," without any regard for consequences or future implications. To share in the glory of Christ, after having endured the unjust suffering, may not even seem like enough of a motivating reason to keep on living. Nevertheless, with the slightest opening of heart to admit even this lack of desire to God, we can find His ear bent to the faintest cry of "being willing to be made willing." God does not expect us to conjure up our own desires any more than He expects us to be able to carry out our obedience or submission to Him! In fact, He knows that we are actually quite incapable of doing so in our own strength! Failure is inevitable when we try to do it on our own. The Good News is that this is exactly how and where He desires to help us—our desires can be literally changed by Him, just as our thoughts, behaviors, and entire lives can be changed by Him too. We were never asked or expected to be strong enough or good enough. Yes, our lives might seem insignificant to us, especially when we try to live in our own strength. But when God breathes His desires and life into our dry places, stand back and be amazed at what all He has in store so as to inspire meaning and deep significance to your life!

You and I each have a unique set of fingerprints, just as we each have a certain mark to make upon this earth. When we give up our own efforts of trying to find it and make it all on our own, and yield to the incredibly glorious power of God to come in and make us whatever He wants us to be, the effects will literally cause us to have the desire to live for a change. Why? Because it's the inspiration of God Almighty—the same Creator of our lives that gave us physical bodies will be, if we allow Him, the same Creator to breathe fresh hope, inspiration, change, and true life to our spiritual bodies (that already have a physical shell in which to dwell)! Do you really think that God would have gone to any effort at all to create us in the first place if we literally didn't matter at all? Of course not. He needed a physical shell to house us, as it were, to accomplish a very specific plan He alone knows.

> "For we are His workmanship [His own master work, a work of art], created in Christ Jesus [reborn from above—spiritually transformed, renewed, ready to be used] for good works, which God prepared [for us] beforehand [taking paths which He set], so that we would walk in them [living the good life which He prearranged and made ready for us]" (Ephesians 2:10 AMP).

So when He created our physical "vehicle" for this certain mission in mind, who are we to take it away by ending our own lives? We would be stepping into the breach between God Almighty as our Creator and the mission that we were made to fill; so interrupting this divine destiny is not a place we would want to be! We need to reverently fear Him too much to encroach upon His territory in this way, leaving us with only one resolve: "Lord, I give up trying to run my own life, including the taking away of it. I am yours to do whatever it is that You have had in mind from the beginning of creating me. I just want to surrender to You at the end of myself now, and let You have Your way."

"For a soul is far too precious to be ransomed by mere earthly wealth. There is not enough of it in all the earth to buy enough for just one soul, to keep it out of hell" (Psalm 49:8-9 TLB). Since this says that a life is far too precious to be ransomed by earthly wealth, wouldn't it also stand to reason that a life is far too precious to extinguish by mere earthly means? Absolutely, your life has immeasurable worth and value, stamped with the validity of God's own Word and marked with His fingerprints upon your heart. He gave you your first breath; please don't casually assume you can breathe your last at your own will. "For it is not an empty or trivial matter for you; indeed it is your very life" (Deuteronomy 32:47a AMP).

"For He will deliver the needy who cry out, the afflicted who have no one to help. He will take pity on the weak and the needy and save the needy from death. He will rescue them from oppression and violence, for precious is their blood in His sight" (Psalm 72:12-14 NIV).

---

1 Romans 8:17

2 Hebrews 12:1-2

3 I Peter 4:13

LAST DAYS

When so many of us thought the year 2020 was the most disturbing year of our lifetime, we had no idea what kinds of chaos, turmoil, and upheaval we would continue to face. With the progression of time, it is simply undeniable that we are living in the end times as prophesied in the Bible.[1]

As the pandemic continued to ravage lives worldwide, we here in America experienced quite a traumatic election process of our United States President, in which it was said that lies, fraudulent activity, and corruption were prevalent. Regardless of your political views, we can all testify about how unsettling it was. After all, even violence erupted at the United States Capitol. Consequentially, our nation has been shifting at a rapid pace into a country we no longer recognize as upholding the values and foundation we knew during our childhoods. Evil is being called good, while good is being called evil.[2] Again, in God's Word, we were warned that this would happen just like it has been unfolding. No one is immune to these effects.

We are not just dealing with major shifting and conflict in the political climate, but history-making winter storms have wreaked havoc on so many people to the equivalent that summer hurricanes have had in the loss of lives and homes. Record breaking weather patterns, fires and floods, even the continual violence and attacks against Israel all point to the imminent return of Jesus. In Daniel 7:25, we read that the enemy seeks to wear out the saints. This is at the core of what is taking place. Are you feeling so worn down that this type of exhaustion and exasperation is driving your temptation of suicide? You are not alone. Many have already taken that path, and families have suffered the greatest heartache of all as a result.

Beloved son or daughter of God, please know that although you may feel alone and crushed underneath the weight of these oppressive circumstances in which we are living, you are definitely not alone; nor are you helpless. We know how the story ends; Jesus is the Victor, and He is fighting *for* you! Just to name one example, the Psalmist David was vehemently threatened and viciously pursued by Saul, who sought to kill him. However, David knew the Source of his strength, help, and deliverance. Countless times, his cries echoed from the lowest depths into the heart of the Lord; and he was consistently triumphant over his enemies all because God's tremendous power was made available to him. After all, we are told that God always causes us to triumph in Jesus Christ![3]

> "Arise, O Lord! O God, lift up Your hand; forget not the humble [patient and crushed]. Why does the wicked [man] condemn (spurn and renounce) God? Why has he thought in his heart, You will not call to account?
>
> You have seen it; yes, You note trouble and grief (vexation) to requite it with Your hand. The unfortunate commits himself to You; You are the helper of the fatherless…
>
> O Lord, You have heard the desire and the longing of the humble and oppressed; You will prepare and strengthen and direct their hearts. You will cause Your ear to hear.
>
> To do justice to the fatherless and the oppressed, so that man, who is of the earth, may not terrify them any more" (Psalm 10:12-14, 17-18).

We are indeed in a crucible where our faith is being tested and tried like never before.[4] Even persecution of Christians is happening in America now as other countries under tyrannical governments have been experiencing already for many years. The point to all this is, God is raising up a remnant who will be loyal to Him no matter what, who will take a righteous stand for truth in the face of opposition, and who will remain faithful to Jesus as our First Love. How kind of God to have forewarned us in His Word of these last days. When Jesus prayed for us in John 17:15, He said that He would "keep and protect us from the evil one." We are safe with Him. Therefore, as the pressures push you into suicide temptation, run to Jesus as your Safe Place, not *away* from Him by taking your life in your own hands.

Yes, these last days are excruciatingly difficult, and life circumstances can prove to be so painful, but we have a Refuge and a Hope in Jesus that anchors our souls, no matter the turbulent times we face.

> "Now we have this hope as a sure and steadfast anchor of the soul [it cannot slip and it cannot break down under whoever steps out upon it—a hope] that reaches farther and enters into [the very certainty of the Presence] within the veil" (Hebrews 6:19 AMP).

> Jesus Himself said, "I have told you these things, so that in Me you may have [perfect] peace and confidence. In the world you have tribulations and trials and distresses and frustration; but be of good cheer [take courage, be confident, certain, undaunted]! For I have overcome the world. [I have deprived it of power to harm you and have conquered it for you]" (John 16:33 AMP).

> "I am with you always, to the very end of the age" (Matthew 28:20 NIV).

He also made it clear that he who overcomes will be given a place with Him, by His side in the throne room of heaven, just as He victoriously overcame and is now seated at God's right hand (Revelation 3:21). In light of this, please don't let anyone steal your crown![5]

You will make it if you do not lose heart and give up. You can do all things through Christ Who strengthens you![6]

1 Mark 13, Matthew 24
2 Isaiah 5:20
3 II Corinthians 2:14
4 I Peter 1:7
5 Revelation 3:11
6 Philippians 4:13

THE GUARANTEED WAY OUT

In this book, I have opened my heart to you as a friend who has truly "been there" in this particular struggle with suicide temptation. Naturally, compassion for you from God Himself has been the ocean from which I've drawn such content as it was born from personal experience as He loved back my own life from the darkness of suicidal struggles. So although it has been in "friend to friend" style of communicating with you on various points that could help you reconsider such a fatal decision, I would be remiss for not ending with summarizing points of your only way out of suicide temptation guaranteed to work every time.

First of all, you need to know with absolute certainty that you are a born-again child of God. If you waver in this assurance, you are welcomed with open-wide, gracious invitation to make it certain! God takes exceptionally good care of His children, and He would love for you to start calling Him your Father. Why this is so important is because every promise of His is meant specifically for those who have personally received His salvation, which we will discuss in a bit. Before moving on though, if you need to begin a new relationship with Jesus by becoming a son or daughter of God for the first time, or by returning from a "far away country" as it were, having lost your way as a prodigal needing to come home, please find the page immediately following this chapter on taking this life-saving step. It is the most important part of the entire book.

Next, know that the Word of God is true life for you. Nothing else whatsoever will ever satisfy. Here is how God expresses it. "Is anyone thirsty? Come and drink—even if you have no money! Come, take your choice of wine or milk—it's all free! Why spend your money on food that does not give you strength? Why pay for food that does you no good? Listen to Me, and you will eat what is good. You will enjoy the finest food. Come to Me with your ears wide open. Listen, and you will find life. I will make an everlasting covenant with you. I will give you all the unfailing love I promised to David" (Isaiah 55:1-3 NLT).

Furthermore, as reserved only for those who are sons and daughters of God (who believe in and have accepted Jesus as Savior and Lord), all the promises of God find their "yes" answer in Jesus Christ. In other words, as one of His very own, and now that you are in progressively closer fellowship with Jesus, you have a right as your inheritance to claim every promise in the Word of God—just for you! What do I mean by this? When you belong to God's family, having been brought near to Him by the Blood of Christ, you can say out loud in times of tormenting fear, anxiety, panic, or powerless feelings, "For God has not given me a spirit of fear; but of power, and of love, and of a sound mind" (II Timothy 1:7 KJV). "But now in Christ Jesus, you who once were far away have been brought near through the blood of Christ" (Ephesians 2:13 NIV). Do you see how personal this all becomes? God's Word is literally for *you!*

Hundreds of verses you can actually claim over your own life as a royal son or daughter of God, Who authored all of His Word for you to have this kind of hope and promise that comes through covenant relationship!

Since you have obtained an inheritance which cannot be shaken, you no longer need to be tormented by fear and anxiety. As a joint heir with Christ, seated with Him in heavenly places, you actually have authority over those powers of darkness which have made you afraid or despairing for so long.¹ You will find that in the atmosphere of God's love and presence, especially as you command your soul to worship Him in spite of how low you feel, your desire to die diminishes as your will to live organically increases. It will be like taking an exhausting swim. Your lungs have been breathing so hard while under water, as such labored breathing has kept you from drowning. Then, when you finally exhaust all your strength and come up for lasting fresh air to sit on the water's edge, you take in such relief as you rest and breathe freely at last.

This brings me to the next point of your guaranteed way out. Make it your number one priority and passion to know the Father heart of God. Discover His love to new heights, greater depths and lengths than ever. Ask Him for an insatiable hunger and thirst to know Him for Who He really is, stripped of all your preconceived ideas or distant opinions that might be drenched in falsehood. Don't settle for just knowing "of Him" in a casual way, but dig deep into His love letter with intensity of hunger and desire. He will meet you this way, I promise. More importantly, He is the One Who has promised this! James 4:7-8 says that if we will submit ourselves to God and resist the enemy, which would mean choosing not to commit suicide, the tormenting enemy absolutely must leave us. Thus, as we draw near to God, He assures us that He will draw near to us. This is when you will find healing happening, because nothing compares to the reward of God's presence. So many times, I remember sobbing my heart out as my entire being wrestled to lay down my will to end my life; but as I decisively surrendered, thereby resisting the enemy, it was not long before the comfort of God's presence drawing near overwhelmed me. That is how it happened for me time after time, until finally the enemy's grip of torment lost its power over me in this area altogether. Give God's presence a chance—once you start drawing nearer to Him, allowing Him to draw nearer to you, the difference it will make in your level of hope and comfort will astound you.

Some good places to begin along these lines are Ephesians 1-3 and 1 John 4:18. Focus your attention and soak your soul on the love of God, which is altogether different than earthly, conditional sources of love that may have left you disillusioned and confused as to what true love really is. In getting to know and internalize God's quality of unconditional love, it is important to let yourself be stripped of all you thought you knew about Him. For instance, if you have only perceived God as a distant disciplinarian, it might be harder for you to receive the actual truth of what He is really like, which is love, love, love! Come empty and broken as you make it your quest to know Him more intimately than ever. Start over with a clean slate of soul if you must, a blank canvas of heart, so that He can show you in His own creative ways that He is actually a good, loving Father—"not harsh, hard, sharp, or pressing" after all (Matthew 11:30 AMP).

Sadly, so many people have a skewed view of God as being punishing or distant, commonly associated with their earthly father experiences. But this is not the case with our Heavenly Father at all. Any wrath of God ended at the Cross when Jesus died for us. That is what made it so powerful. Jesus actually bore our punishment, once and for all, incurring the wrath of God against sin, to spare us of having to be punished. That's the reason it was so hard for Jesus when He was agonizing to the point of sweating blood as He prayed in the Garden of Gethsemane if there be any other way for the cup of suffering God's wrath to pass from Him. It wasn't that He was hesitant to suffer for us. As hard as that was, He was so willing. What was by far the hardest part of it though was knowing He would experience separation from His Father once the crushing weight of all our sin would bear down upon Him. Remember, that is what sin does—it causes separation from God. But you see, Jesus experienced that horror so that we wouldn't have to. This finished work that Jesus accomplished made it possible for us to have direct access to God at any time, because the veil was torn. "In Him and through faith in Him we may approach God with freedom and confidence" (Ephesians 3:12 NIV).

The Blood of Jesus is, and always has been, a tremendously powerful agent that destroyed the hostile dividing wall. Through His own Body, Jesus made peace for us. Whereas Jews had always been God's chosen people, Jesus' death and resurrection enabled Gentiles to be grafted into the same inheritance. You can read about this more in Ephesians 2:13-22. Understand that you no longer have to live under a cloud of heavy labels—"disqualified, rejected, or not good enough." God makes Himself fully accessible, never distant, and is actually wanting to be as intimately connected with you insofar as you are willing and desiring the same.

He is such an incredibly good Father! Make it your ambition and burning passion to know Him better. As you do, you will truly find the tormenting temptation to end your life loosening its painful grip on you. Since I wanted to die for so long, I didn't even know what it was like to *want* to live. I will never forget what it felt like to realize for the first time in years that I actually wanted to live for a change. This is what I yearn for you to experience. It is what your Heavenly Father wants for you too. His heart breaks with you as you suffer under this crushing weight of sorrow. The enemy is such a cruel, driving taskmaster, pursuing you with hatred and vengeance because he seeks anyone he can seize and devour. His motive is to kill, steal, and destroy. God's motive is to love you back to life and restore your will to live, since His plans and purposes for you are only of peace, a hope for your future—not harm.[2]

God's love is the most healing ingredient known to man. We were created for love. God is not angry with you at all. Even if you have committed criminal offenses, or struggle with some secretive besetting sin of which you are deeply ashamed and feel powerless to quit, God still loves you and is not mad at you. In fact, He doesn't even expect you to change on your own, because you can't! None of us can! Freedom and hope all begin with His love. Don't even worry about trying to change your shameful habits or make yourself "better" on your own. It is futility to put forth such human effort. Simply begin with coming broken before God and allowing His love to pour into you. Come empty and depleted as you are. That is what He loves to fill, heal, and restore. "He Who began a good work in you will carry it on to completion" (Philippians 1:6 NIV). It all starts with receiving His unconditional love. This is your guaranteed way out.

Ask God for a deeper hunger to understand His Word, and to find your identity in Christ. Soak in Ephesians and Hebrews for all the freedom you crave, but haven't been able to attain on your own. Explore the book of John, full of stories to show what Jesus was like when He was on earth as a human being, how and why people were so drawn to Him. Take comfort in the Psalms, as the primary author knew struggles with depression to the depths, yet found hope every time in God. You will identify with his words and cries as if they were your own, and it will trace you towards hope and peace as well. Absorb the book of Proverbs for the wisdom you need to navigate through tough decisions. Are you getting the idea? "The Word is a lamp for your feet and a light for your path" (Psalm 119:105). Listening to an audio Bible also may help soothe your nerves, calm your fears, and breathe hope into your dry places, as "faith comes by hearing the Word" (Romans 10:17).

What you may perceive to be oversimplified really isn't at all. We make the Gospel much more complicated than it was ever meant to be. Jesus said that unless we become like little children, we will not enter the Kingdom of Heaven (Matthew 18:3). One thing children know how to do extremely well is to receive! A classic illustration Jesus uses is to picture a good, earthly father giving a stone to a child who had asked for some bread. It would never happen! Your Father in heaven gave you the gift of life—not for you to despise it or take it in your own hands and destroy it. He wants you to enjoy the gift that it truly is. Again, when you internalize His love, even during times of life that are extremely hard with loss or struggle, you will discover that life really is a gift each and every day. In this life, God actually wants to prosper you and bless you—not punish you! Here is a snapshot of how God feels towards you.

> "And therefore the Lord earnestly waits [expecting, looking, and longing] to be gracious to you; and therefore He lifts Himself up, that He may have mercy on you and show loving-kindness to you. For the Lord is a God of justice. Blessed (happy, fortunate, to be envied) are all those who [earnestly] wait for Him, who expect and look and long for Him [for His victory, His favor, His love, His peace, His joy, and His matchless, unbroken companionship]!...He will surely be gracious to you at the sound of your cry; when He hears it, He will answers you. And though the Lord gives you the bread of adversity and the water of affliction, yet your Teacher will not hide Himself any more, but your eyes will constantly behold your Teacher. And your ears will hear a word behind you, saying, 'This is the way; walk in it, when you turn to the right hand and when you turn to the left'" (Isaiah 30:18-21 AMP).

Do you see how much God is actually yearning to lavish His love and goodness on you? It's true! His love in all its fullness is the guaranteed way out of despair. Does this sound oversimplified to the point of ridiculous to you as the most reliable answer? Let me take you a little deeper into a specific example from my own life as to how this worked.

I thought I knew the love of God. I had grown up in church and had such a precious heritage. My mom and grandparents were deeply devoted to the Lord and exuded His love in such a great way. So the subject of God's love seemed basic, simple, and easy to believe. Little did I know over time, however, that experiencing life's disappointments, trauma and abuse, other hurts and heartache had opened the door to doubt and unbelief of His love in ways not so readily detected until I was so far gone into a full blown stronghold of being convinced God could not possibly love me. This took years to untangle the lies and rebuild a foundation of truth.

From the abusive situation shared in an earlier chapter that had such heavily dark influences and destruction to my self-concept, I found myself in the victim role later in life in a repetitive cycle. Yet it all began with that early experience that shook my foundation with the unhealthy, wrong and delusional spiritual undertones that initially marred my perception of God and eroded so much of what I had grown up knowing about Him. I felt utterly ruined, destroyed, as if I was damaged goods. Thus, in the following years, it seemed like I never could get back on my feet in terms of confidence, hope, or joy.

The pervasive struggles with suicidal depression, anxiety, and anorexia/bulimia proved extremely difficult to overcome. My entire personhood was so broken down that I was gaunt, with hollow eyes of hopelessness, and had deteriorated so much over time that I no longer recognized myself; neither did family or friends. The many years that were spent in counseling, residential treatment centers, and seeking God's Word for recovery was a process which continually circled around the love of God as the central theme of my journey.

The problems I had with rage, self-mutilation, all sorts of self-destructive behaviors caused me to crash repeatedly into the unconditional nature of God's love. It was as if I was trying hard to convince Him not to love me, or to prove that I was unlovable. This never worked! His love was inescapable. God was every bit as determined to keep loving me unconditionally as I was evidently convinced He should give up on me. This was a living, breathing exchange that endured through such dark nights of my soul as I tried to wrestle and work through the recovery process of becoming whole. Eventually, God's love won my war.

Once I began yielding to His love instead of fighting it, profound differences began taking place. Actually receiving His love, literally internalizing it and allowing it to affect us at every level of living, is vastly different than just head knowledge. I truly discovered His heart of unconditional love that was ultimately proven at the Cross, but has been actively displayed and carried out all these years later to ones so undeserving as we all are. Yes, it is absolutely the guaranteed way out when we start receiving and personally internalizing this passionate, unconditional love of our Father—totally apart from what we have done or how dark and shameful our current struggles may be.

Maybe you relate to the worthlessness I was feeling about myself which manifested in various destructive behaviors. My friend, let me assure you of your worth in your Heavenly Father's eyes. It extends higher, deeper, longer, and wider than you can imagine. Perhaps you are living what I described about my darkest years, allowing the enemy to feed you lies that your life doesn't matter or that there is no way out of your pain. Subconsciously, you are feeding on falsehood, putting more faith in your fears of never measuring up to a God you feel you can never please, than faith in His love. Please allow Him a chance to show you otherwise. When we feed on the enemy's lies that His love wavers and wanes, or has unattainable conditions, we stifle the experience of God revealing His glory to us. Picture a gorgeous sunset, radiant and aglow with brilliant orange, pink, and magenta hues; but when you draw your curtains across the window, you can no longer see the beauty. It's still there, altogether glorious and awe inspiring, but you are missing it because you are sitting behind closed curtains that block such a picturesque view. Our experience of God's love and overall character is similar. He continues loving (it is truly Who He is); and He still shows incredible grace to all sorts of undeserving people. But when we have blinders of doubting His love over our eyes, as it were, we cannot see such truth or experience it even though it is very much there, like the gorgeous sunset.

This is what happened with me, as I described earlier. My doubts of God's love became so blinding that I no longer believed He could possibly love me, and that is exactly how despair developed such an oppressive stronghold on my life. As a result, I was tempted to commit suicide. Is this where you are? There is hope for you!

Once I hit the proverbial brick wall of desperation, I essentially started over in seeking to know God. It required being stripped of all I thought I knew, as well as emptying myself of all the garbage full of lies. This involved renewing my mind and being washed with the water of the Word.[3] Caught between suicide temptation and the fear of not succeeding, I gave God a chance to redeem my mess of a ruined life. Essentially, I began at square one in getting to know God for Who He really is. Little by little, over a period of time in which I sought Him through reading the Word, getting in a church with a solid foundation in the Bible and one that was open to the flow of His Holy Spirit, spending every spare minute I could to read and explore more of His character, hope began stirring. Playing worship music and fully engaging with it, letting the weight of God's glory blanket me, literally cleansed the atmosphere, while also washing all over me with peace. The enemy cannot stand this; he is forced to go. Fear and torment absolutely cannot share the same dwelling place with God's strong presence. How to get rid of torment? Worship God, Who is Love!

In these ways, despair eventually lost its grip on me altogether. I began walking out of the dark shadows of hopelessness into the light of His presence, which kept proving so inviting and warm. What hope this gave me! Remember, my destructive behaviors did not change overnight by any means! But this was exactly how I discovered just how unconditional God's love really was! I had no perfection of my own with which to justify His love! It was in my utter brokenness that His love became so piercingly real and personal to me. Internalizing it was key.

Over time, it even challenged and changed my self-image from being derogatory and punitive to being esteemed and valued by God as He enabled me to see myself through His eyes. Healthy desires and perspectives mushroomed from there, such as wanting His will for my life (since I learned they really were good plans of hope and peace, not of harm or evil); as opposed to my stubborn lament of wanting to end my life. This can happen for you too. Begin with giving Him your will to die, your suicide temptation, and letting Him have His way with your heart. Cry out to Him that you really do want to believe and experience His love in a real, personal way. When you lay down your will one night and invite Him to come in a very present way, see what happens. You will find Him responding to you in ways you never thought possible. As the next night comes, and then the next, do it again. One day at a time is all you need to focus on. Keep inviting Him into your messed up, broken life. Wait in the atmosphere of worship. He hears you crying and whispers, "Be still, and know that I am God" (Psalm 46:10). It may seem unbearably painful at first just to be so still and quiet as you lay down your temptations and will to end your life. However, you will be rewarded by a sense of His strong, loving presence that will make it all worth the pain. You just have to give Him a chance though. He is too gentle and kind to force Himself on you. Isn't this amazing? He actually honors the fact that He gave us a free will, and therefore will not violate it. He waits on us to lay down our will, come empty-handed and broken to Him, and invite Him into our painful place. Jesus literally said, "I will never reject anyone" (John 6:37 AMP). I promise, and more importantly, Jesus promises that He will never, ever reject you, leave or forsake you.[4]

Deeply internalizing the love of God for yourself personally will undoubtedly prove life-changing. Because Jesus is the Light and Life of all men, and came full of grace and truth, you just may be surprised to find that experiencing relationship with Him on an intimate, hourly basis each day will completely erase your despairing death wish. Give Him time to reveal Himself to you. He has so much to say to you, full of love, hope, and purpose. He wants to infuse your life with meaning. Nothing compares with His presence. Let Him give you life in its true, abundant form.[5] Allow Him to love you by way of restoring your soul.[6] He offers to give you beauty for ashes and joy for mourning.[7] So it's time to pull back the curtains and let the radiance of that gorgeous sunshine fill your dark room with bursting beauty and light! In a very real sense, this is what you are doing as you open your darkened heart to the hope of His light and love. Always remember, God loves you so deeply and extravagantly. You can never go beyond the reaches of His love! "There is no pit so deep that God's love is not deeper still."[8]

"In Him we have redemption through His blood, the forgiveness of sins, in accordance with the riches of God's grace that He lavished on us with all wisdom and understanding…In Him we were also chosen, having been predestined according to the plan of Him who works out everything in conformity with the purpose of His will…When you believed, you were marked in Him with a seal, the promised Holy Spirit, who is a deposit guaranteeing our inheritance…" (Ephesians 1:7-8,11-14 NIV).

"For this reason, ever since I heard about your faith in the Lord Jesus…I have not stopped giving thanks for you, remembering you in my prayers. I keep asking that the God of our Lord Jesus Christ, the glorious Father, may give you the Spirit of wisdom and revelation, so that you may know Him better. I pray that the eyes of your heart may be enlightened in order that you may know the hope to which He has called you, the riches of His glorious inheritance in His holy people, and His incomparably great power for us who believe. That power is the same as the mighty strength He exerted when He raised Christ from the dead and seated Him at His right hand in the heavenly realms, far above all rule and authority, power and dominion, and every name that is invoked, not only in the present age but also in the one to come. And God placed all things under His feet and appointed Him to be head over everything for the church, which is His body, the fullness of Him Who fills everything in every way" (Ephesians 1:15-22 NIV).

Because of His great love for us, God, Who is rich in mercy, made us alive with Christ even when we were dead in transgressions—it is by grace you have been saved. And God raised us up with Christ and seated us with Him in the heavenly realms in Christ Jesus, in order that in the coming ages He might show the incomparable riches of His grace, expressed in His kindness to us in Christ Jesus. For it is by grace you have been saved, through faith—and this not from yourselves, it is the gift of God—not by works, so that no one can boast. For we are God's handiwork, created in Christ Jesus to do good works, which God prepared in advance for us to do" (Ephesians 2:4-10 NIV).

"For this reason I kneel before the Father, from Whom His whole family in heaven and on earth derives its name. I pray that out of His glorious riches He may strengthen you with power through His Spirit in your inner being, so that Christ may dwell in your hearts through faith. And I pray that you, being rooted and established in love, may have power, together with all the saints, to grasp how wide and long and high and deep is the love of Christ, and to know this love that surpasses knowledge—that you may be filled to the measure of all the fullness of God. Now to Him Who is able to do immeasurably more than all we ask or imagine, according to His power that is at work within us, to Him be glory in the church and in Christ Jesus throughout all generations, for ever and ever! Amen" (Ephesians 3:14-21 NIV).

---

1 Ephesians 2:6

2 Jeremiah 29:11

3 Romans 12:1-2; Ephesians 5:26

4 Hebrews 13:5

5 John 10:10

6 Psalm 23:3

7 Isaiah 61:3

8 Ten Boom, Corrie; Sherrill, John and Elizabeth. *The Hiding Place*. (Uhrichsville, OH: Barbour and Company, Inc., 1971), 197.

SECTION THREE

PRAYER FOR SALVATION

Jesus,

I have come to the realization that I need You in every desperate way. There is no way I can go on even one more hour without You.

You have been the Light to shine into my dark places, showing me how utterly wretched I am without You. I repent of all the ways I've sinned against You. There is no self-righteousness I can offer, as my own self-righteousness is as filthy rags in Your eyes anyway. It is only by Your precious Blood that You shed for me that will cleanse me from sin and despair, and save my soul for eternity with You. Thank You, Jesus, for dying for me so that I can be forgiven.

Your Word says that if I confess my sins to You, You are faithful and just to forgive me, and to cleanse me from all unrighteousness (I John 1:9). So I humble myself before You, asking not only for Your forgiveness, but inviting You to come into my heart to be my Savior and Lord.

I believe in You, Jesus, that You are the only Way, Truth and Life. No one can come to the Father but through You (John 14:6). I receive this truth wholeheartedly.

Just like You said as the Good Shepherd that You leave the ninety-nine to go after the one who was lost, that's me. Thank You with all my heart for knowing where I am, for rescuing and saving me from the dark places, and giving me hope and a reason to live.

I receive Your peace, not as the world gives, but Your own peace that You promised to me; so that I don't have to let my heart be troubled or afraid anymore (John 14:1, 27). My life is safe with You in an everlasting way now. Thank You for taking such good care of Your own!

I love You with all my heart and want You to show me what my life's purpose is going forward. Give me a deep hunger to know You for Who You really are, and to understand Your Word as the only Bread that truly satisfies. Breathe life into my dry bones so I can begin to live the abundant life You promised, and enjoy Your sweet, intimate presence for the rest of my days.

In Jesus' name I pray,

Amen!

Congratulations! All of heaven roars with rejoicing when you come home to God's heart and receive His love and salvation! Be sure to tell someone that you've made this huge turning point, as well as share the Good News with someone else who needs it. You have a purpose-filled life now!

NOTES TO THE OTHERS INVOLVED

Perhaps you picked up this book not because you are the one struggling with suicide temptation, but you are searching for a way to help someone else who is. It may also be that you are grappling with grief, blaming yourself, and baited with depression if your loved one already succeeded with suicide. This chapter is for you.

Years later, when my mom admitted her true human emotions in regards to this struggle of mine, specifically referencing the chapter, "Your Shift Is Coming," she shared how afraid she really did feel, along with helplessness, guilt, and full of questions ("Why? What have I done wrong? What should I have done differently?" and others). In that particular chapter's example of her resilience, it was important to note that she was acting out the truth presented of what I had to do myself. That is, she was also evidently aware that her words had power in speaking life over me to refute the death that was gripping my life. Although she actually was afraid, she did not act or speak in fear; because the enemy gains all the more ground when we cave into his fear-provoking tactics, as if to feed him the satisfaction that his lies are working. He studies our responses; and I'm grateful to say that her response to fear was faith. Her opposing response to my falsehood and manipulation, such as when I was threatening suicide, was the truth of God's Word. Her way of combating my sobbing admittance to shame I was feeling was to love me unconditionally and boldly in the face of my worst verbal rages over the phone, as well as to pray the perfect love of God into my ear. Instead of inducing guilt for the act of suicide that I was threatening, she might have said a phrase or two such as, "Well, that will crush me; but it's your choice"; yet her own words like these were few, as she would intuitively begin pleading the Blood of Jesus over my life and commanding every foul spirit of death and suicide to leave me at once in Jesus' mighty Name.

From her own words, she revealed her own underlying struggles. "When I would get extremely afraid that you were going to die—either from the slow suicide of anorexia or a sudden, drastic act of taking your life, it was almost more than I could handle. Then God would remind me that He loved His own Son enough to surrender. So even if it meant that I would grieve, I knew I had to place you in His hands and give you completely to Him; otherwise, I was making you an idol. He alone is the One I was to fear in every worshipful way. To fear your death so much would distract me from focusing on Him as the One I loved most of all. It was in this excruciating place of surrender that His peace would always come; though I had to repeat this process more than once."

None of these are pat answers, as there are not any to offer anyway. This is a situation in which I have overwhelming empathy and compassion, with no trace of judgment, criticism, or condemnation whatsoever. After all, if you have lost a loved one by way of suicide, you have far enough pain and grief in your loss already. You cannot and must not take on guilt and shame. My mother was right in that it was my choice, just like it was your loved one's choice also. No matter the emotion you feel, you have every right to feel it; because it is yours, be it anger, confusion, shock, resentment, profound sadness and grief, or any others. These are all natural, and no two people are alike; tragedy of any kind can affect us all differently, especially this one wherein your relationship dynamics with your lost loved one might inevitably be analyzed. The truth is, no one can take the blame, even if that was the explicit threat; because again, each of us has to make our own individual choices in life. Never give up or beat yourself up, nor take any blame or shame. God is *for* you. Even though you walk through the valley of the shadow of death, you do not have to fear any evil; for He has promised to be with you (Psalm 23:4).

My heart breaks for you just as much as for your loved one, whether tragedy has already occurred, or you have picked up this book in hopes to prevent it from happening. Know that Jesus is the safest place to run with all your fears, heartache, and suffering. He provides our only hope as a sure and steadfast anchor of the soul (Hebrews 6:19). In God, you can find refuge and strength, for He is your very present help in times of trouble (Psalm 46:1). He can handle your strongest emotions with great ease, and has all the comfort you need in return. My prayer for you is that He becomes your hiding place, surrounding you with songs and shouts of deliverance, counseling you and watching over you as the tender, loving Father that He is (Psalm 32:7-8).

When I lost a loved one whom I loved most of all, the most meaningful verse I held onto with all my heart is the one I leave with you in closing. "Be strong and courageous. Do not be terrified or dismayed (intimidated), for the Lord your God is with you wherever you go" (Joshua 1:9 AMP). Not counting extended family or friends, I've had nine losses in my lifetime, five of which had an especially profound effect, as I was so close to them. One was actually my mom, who died a few years ago as I finally finish this project that she knew about and encouraged me to complete. From the contents of this book, you have gotten a glimpse as to the integral part she had, as I clearly would not be here had it not been for her intercessory prayers throughout my life. Even in the years that I was a prodigal, estranged, and felt too dark to pray effectively, I took great comfort and refuge in knowing my mom was in God's Throne-room interceding for me on a daily basis. The same effect can happen through you for your struggling loved one. It's why I included it in this book. Your prayers hold powerful sway against the kingdom of darkness; never lose sight of this or give up.

If your loved one is already gone, I weep with you and feel your pain, which is why I draw the connection of loss here. I understand how devastatingly hard it is. There is no easy formula; it takes time to heal and likely won't be overnight, especially when you've been so traumatized. However, there is a guaranteed way out for you as well. Jesus was acquainted with grief Himself. Whereas I am limited in my understanding, since I don't even know your name, He is fully aware and does know your name, including the full story of your pain. He has promised to heal the brokenhearted and be close to you.

"God will wipe away every tear from [your] eyes; and death shall be no more, neither shall there be anguish (sorrow and mourning), nor grief nor pain anymore…" (Revelation 21:4 AMPC).

ABOUT THE AUTHOR

Glena earned her Bachelor of Arts in Sociology and Psychology through Stephen F. Austin State University in Nacogdoches, Texas, and is currently pursuing graduate studies in counseling. Beyond education, however, she has overcome numerous obstacles to achieve her current place of freedom. Having struggled relentlessly with suicidal depression, anxiety, and addictive cycles, she writes from a wealth of experience for those seeking recovery.

With a special anointing to reach hurting, bound, and broken people, Glena utilizes her strong command of God's Word to show that Jesus came to set the captives free and give us life abundantly. She ministers the love of God in a dynamic teaching style, causing the Word to come alive as it communicates God's heart of compassion to the vulnerable, weak, and wounded.

Restoration of lives is her passion, sharing from experience that no one is beyond His redemptive reach, even to create purpose from trauma, suffering, failure, and loss. Through her love for writing and employment with a worldwide Christian ministry organization, Glena actively encourages those who are struggling that there is *always* hope in Jesus!

www.ingramcontent.com/pod-product-compliance
Lightning Source LLC
Chambersburg PA
CBHW031245290426
44109CB00012B/440